Time
Management

Smart Hacks To Get Things Done, Stop Procrastination
Habit And Increase Focus And Productivity

David Tracy & Brian Allen

Published by Jason Thawne Publishing House

© David Tracy & Brian Allen

Time Management: Smart Hacks To Get Things Done,
Stop Procrastination Habit And Increase
Focus And Productivity

ISBN 978-1-989749-11-1

TABLE OF CONTENTS

This document is geared towards providing exact and reliable information in regards to the topic and issue covered. The publication is sold with the idea that the publisher isn't required to render accounting, officially permitted, or otherwise, qualified services. If advice is necessary, legal or even professional, a practiced individual in the profession should be ordered.

- From a Declaration of Principles which was accepted and approved equally by a Committee of the American Bar Association and a Committee of Publishers and Associations.

The information provided herein is stated to be truthful and consistent, in that any liability, in terms of inattention or otherwise, by any usage or abuse of any policies, processes, or directions contained within is the solitary and also utter responsibility of the recipient reader. Under no circumstances will any legal responsibility or blame be held against the publisher for any reparation, damages, or monetary loss due to the information herein, either directly or indirectly.

Respective authors own all copyrights not held by the publisher.

The information herein is offered for just informational purposes solely, and is universal as so. The presentation of the information is without contract or any type of guarantee assurance.

The trademarks that are used are without any consent, and also the publication of the trademark is without permission or backing by the trademark owner. All trademarks and brands within this book are for clarifying purposes only and are the owned by the owners themselves, not affiliated with this document.

Chapter 1: Time Management And Its Importance

What is time management?

It is a set of principles, practices, skills, tools and systems that help you use your time to accomplish what you want.

Why is time management important?

Time management is important for your personal life and career success. It teaches you how to manage your time effectively and make the most of it.

Here are a few of the reasons why it is so important, and how it can help you use and manage your time more advantageously:

1. Time is a special resource that you cannot store or save for later use. Everyone has the exact same amount of time each day. Time not well used cannot be retrieved.

2. Most people, feel like they have too much to do and not enough time. They blame lack of time for their poor finances, stress, bad relationships, and for not exercising their body.

Wise time management can help you find the time for what you desire, and for what you need to do.

3. You need time to get what you want out of life. If you wait for extra time to appear, you might lose the game of life. Through

right time management, you can"create"the time you need, and not just wait for it to come. By planning your time wisely, you will have more time to do more things.

4. Time management will help you set up your priorities.

5. Time is limited to 24 hours a day, so plan your life wisely.

6. Time management helps you make conscious choices, so you can spend more of your time doing things that are important and valuable to you.

7. You can learn to find the time for the things that are important to you. Even a small amount of time once a day, or even once a week, will take you closer to your goals, and you will be surprised at the progress you make.

8. You become more productive using improved time management skills and tools, and can accomplish more with less effort and time. Time management can help you reduce wasted time and energy, help you become more creative and

productive, and enable you to do the right thing at the right time. This will of course lead to more balance and fulfillment in your life.

9. Life today presents so many distractions, and therefore, it is very easy to lose time on unimportant activities. Ask yourself, is watching this or that TV program, reading this or that gossip or participating in a certain activity is going to add anything to your life. Is the time spent on a particular activity well spent, or is just a waste of time and energy?

10. Life puts in front of everyone so many choices each day, and the question is, do you follow what appears on your way, or do you consciously choose what you want to do? Do you allow external distractions to deter you from your goal, or do you use willpower and self -discipline to walk toward your goal in a straight line, without wasting time and energy?

11. A certain degree of detachment and inner peace are useful in managing your time effectively. They help you avoid spending too much emotional and mental

energy on what people say and think about you. They help you stay calm, despite distractions or difficulties, and this saves you a lot of time and energy, which you can spend on better and more rewarding activities.

There are many things you can do and tools to use to manage your time effectively. There is a lot of time wasted each day, which can be put to better uses. There are changes you can make, which will effectively increase the time you have at your disposal every day.

Thinking, planning, finding out how others manage their time, and reading books and articles on time management, will develop these skills and give you good ideas.

Among the many changes that you can make to manage your time, there is one that is important and easily available, and that is getting up early in the morning. Give up watching TV late at night and go to sleep a little earlier than usual. It will then be easier to wake up earlier.

Even waking up only 15 minutes earlier would be great. It is a time of quietude, before everyone else wakes up, which you can devote to reading, meditating, exercising, or planning your day.

To get rid of the feeling that you have much to do and not enough time, try to feel and to think, as if you have all the time in the world.

This kind of thinking would enable you to focus on what you are doing, without stress and strain.

Always plan your time well and don't waste it on useless matters. Be careful not to procrastinate, and do everything in the best way you can, with focus and attention.

Chapter 2: The Iconic Mcdonald's System

"We should work on our process, not the outcome of our process."
— W. Edwards Deming

McDonald's has 36,525 restaurants around the globe. They are found in 118 countries and serve 68 million customers each day. That's around one percent of world's population, every single day. Mind blowing.

McDonald's employs half a million people, most of whom, as you probably know, are acne-ridden high school kids.

But here is the most amazing part: Despite the massive scale and complexity of this multinational corporation, their product and service is consistent.

I could go to a McDonald's store in the United States, then the United Kingdom, and then in Australia, and everything would be the same. I would get the same food. I would get the same service. The store would look the same. Everything.

Even more staggering is that most McDonald's employees are failing high school students.

How is it that McDonald's, in all its 36,525 stores, is perfectly consistent — especially when its employees are mostly incompetent?

Here's how: McDonald's has a secret. They are perhaps the best in the world at creating systems. They break down all aspects of the business into their simplest components. They reduce their entire business to no more than a collection of little steps. They make these small steps so simple that a bunch of failing high school kid can run the business. Literally.

McDonald's builds a simple, step by step process. They then turn it over to their employees. The result of this system is that you get the exact same experience no matter what McDonald's store you go to — an extraordinarily impressive feat considering they hire some of the least skilled workers in the world.

So let's take a look at what the "McDonald's system" can teach us about time management.

The General and the Troops

Most people work long and hard, but fail to work smart. The biggest hurdle to working smart is indecision and lack of direction. This is because we humans have two modes of work: Strategizing and doing. We plan and we act.

The problem is that we often try to do both of these things at the same time. One minute we are in "go mode," the next minute we are in "strategy mode." This not only slows us down and makes us highly inefficient, but it leads to multitasking and decision fatigue.

Multitasking causes a 40 percent drop in efficiency. Decision fatigue depletes one's willpower. Decision fatigue also, as its name suggests, reduces the quality of subsequent decisions.

So what's the solution?

This dilemma can be resolved by dedicating a block of time to being in "strategy mode." This frees up the rest of one's time for being in "go mode." This clear division eliminates the need for multitasking. It also extinguishes the decision fatigue that saps at one's willpower and reduces the quality of one's work.

The effectiveness of an army would be severely limited if men were required to fill both the role of the general and the infantry.

The quality of an essay would be severely limited if one could not draw up an outline.

The insight offered by an academic paper would be severely limited were it not researched and planned.

The potential success of a business would be severely limited if no business plan were to be produced.

The ability of a film to engage and captivate audiences would be severely limited if the director had no script.

The safety of passenger jets would be severely limited if pilots never had takeoff checklists.

The utility of an airplane as a method of transport would be severely limited were there no flight plans.

It's clear, isn't it? "Strategy mode" and "go mode" must be disentangled from one another. One cannot direct a film without already having a script. One cannot write an effective academic paper without prior research and planning. One cannot be both general and soldier.

To maximize efficiency, one must set aside a block of time dedicated to being the general — "strategy mode." Then one can return to the battlefield as a soldier — "go mode" — free of strategy-related worries.

By disentangling these two roles, one can mindlessly power through stacks of complex work without so much as a single thought. This is efficiency at its best. It's the beauty of working smart.

As success coach Brian Tracy said, "Every minute you spend in planning saves 10 minutes in execution; this gives you a 1,000 percent Return on Energy!"

You can't be both CEO and employee at the same time. You can't be both general and soldier at the same time. Separate the two roles and your efficiency will go through the roof. You must work smart.

Utilizing the Process

The first step to utilizing the "McDonald's system" is to set aside one day each week for intense planning. You will spend this time planning the week or so.

Although it might seem rather extreme to be spending this much time on planning, remember that the more detail that goes into planning, the less time you will end up wasting during the week. As Brian Tracy said in the aforementioned quote, "Every minute you spend in planning saves 10 minutes in execution." Sounds like a good deal to me.

Furthermore, you will eventually become faster. You'll end up being able to plan the next week in a single afternoon (or evening) at the end of the weekend.

Keep in mind that it is important to not include any more than five major goals or projects.

Now, the second step is to break these goals into smaller tasks — sub-projects.

For the third step, make sure to go into "McDonald's level" detail on your sub-projects. Make it so simple that an ance-ridden failing high school kid could do it. You want to make it so that you don't have to think about what it is that you're doing. You can just go, go, go without needing to stop and think too much. You want to work with machine-like efficiency.

The fourth step is to determine how long each task will take and assign time frames. It might take an entire day, half a day, or a quarter of a day. Be a little conservative. It's better to have a little time left over than to be forced to completely abandon your plan.

Finally, the fifth step is to print your plan out and stick it to your desk. This plan is to you what a map is to a sailor. With this plan, you'll be free to focus exclusively on taking action — being in "go mode" — for the next week or so. No more worrying about what the next step is or constantly switching between "strategy mode" and "go mode."

By embracing the "McDonald's system" and disentangling the roles of general and soldier, you eliminate decision fatigue, boost energy levels, and skyrocket your efficiency.

The creation of such a roadmap by laying out the process — the little steps — enables clockwork-like productivity. Just like in a mechanical clock, all the little parts work together to create a perfectly predictable outcome.

Process vs Outcome

There two ways one can operate:

1. Focus on the outcome.
2. Focus on the process.

As you likely know, most people focus exclusively on the outcome. This can be handy in "strategy mode," however, if it persists throughout other stages of work — such as "go mode" — this obsessive focus on the outcome can, ironically, become detrimental to the outcome.

Measuring yourself against short-term results is a terrible strategy. The key to effective time management and the consequent jaw-dropping productivity is to determine the actions that lead to the long-term results you desire.

Focus on the process, not the outcome. You have zero control over the outcome. What you do have control over, however, is the process. Adjust the process and the results you are getting will change accordingly. Just focusing on the outcome will not move you any nearer to that which you are striving for.

Chapter 3: Never Begin The Day With An Apology

Fashionably late is for celebrities; you'll just end up saying Sorry

Laugh and the world laughs with you, be prompt and you dine alone.

-Gerald Barzan

Here's a little test. Think back and determine how often you start your day with "I apologize for being late..."

Is sorry the first word you use every day? Imagine how your day would progress if it begins with an apology – and that for something as irresponsible as being late! Think of yourself as this harried individual who's always rushing into meetings, the last person to sit at the conference table. Someone who's forever embarrassed, whose papers are always flying, blaming the watch. The one whom others grumble about for keeping them back. Would you like to work with a person like that? Would anyone?

How you keep time mirrors your personality. It is been proven that punctual people also show character and integrity, as against latecomers who tend to be casual about everything. It may look like a minor issue – just a matter of being delayed by five minutes – but it could be indicative of a larger problem, the proverbial tip of the iceberg.

It is quite possible: You don't realize the fact that you are a chronic latecomer. What to do then? First, acknowledge that tardiness is a problem that you need to tackle, because awareness is where change begins. Next, take the necessary steps to counter it. Why waste time? Make a new beginning right away.

Punctuality – make it a priority

Often, lateness turns out to be a habit learned in childhood. Hence it takes more than just a wish to be punctual. It requires a complete attitudinal change. And this change involves the clock. Earlier, you looked at it only when you were running late. Now you need make it the center of you attention through the day.

Put in on paper, commit to it

Take a piece of paper and jot down every activity you need to get done for that day. Against each, mark the time required and the hour on the clock you'd attempt to do it. Then you go about accomplishing them, one task at a time. Keep a close watch on the time you take on each, and the hour you do it. Close monitoring is the only other way. There's tremendous joy in ticking off tasks on a list! So let the watch drive your day rather than frenzy.

Don't cram it with stuff:

When you make your list, don't be too ambitious. We're trying to solve a problem here, not running a marathon. So get real, and get going. Again, use the Urgent-Important technique (see previous chapter) to prioritize your list. Accomplish less, that's fine, as long as you do it well. With practice, you can start adding more tasks and eventually you'll master the art of doing more, and in time.

When scheduling meetings, less is more:

The same rule applies at work. Just attending meetings is no sign of efficiency if nothing concrete comes out of them. The same applies with appointments. It is good to be a busybody but it is better to be an achiever. This is why it makes sense to have fewer meetings that are more productive than have a chockfull day with nothing achieved in the end.

Understand that meetings don't end on time:

How often have you sat at the tail of a meeting worrying if you ever get to the next one on time? This is precisely why you shouldn't stack your appointments back to back. As meetings telescope into each other, people across the board get upset that you are late, causing stress and angry reactions. Not only that – it cements your notoriety further as a chronic latecomer who can't be trusted with time.

Before fixing a meeting – do you need a meeting?

Meetings have become the bane of the corporate world. Executives need to be seen as busy, so the easiest way out is to fix meetings - discussing with other department colleagues, rushing in and out of cabins and pretending to work. So ask yourself: Does this task warrant a meeting? If it is just a Yes or No that you seek as an answer, do you really need to meet the person? Often, a call or a short mail is all it takes. You save a lot of time, which can be used for other tasks.

Expect things to get delayed during the day:

If you anticipate something, you are mentally prepared for it. When you expect the unexpected you are accepting that things don't always go like clockwork, and that sometimes there will be genuine traffic jams and colleagues who fall ill. Account for such unavoidable occurrences in life. However, if you plan for them and set aside time in advance, no delay happens or when it does it won't affect the workflow.

Avoid distractions that delay you:

Today, it is common to engross yourself in one or the other gadgets — be it watching videos on YouTube or chatting with friends on the cell phone. Though most people indulge in these to de-stress themselves (and a good thing too), you'll not realize how and when the gadgets take control over you and your time. Make no mistake, a gadget can make your life simpler and more efficient however, you often end up becoming its slave. In turn you become a hapless victim to its many attractions, taking your mind away from critical tasks at hand. Delays result.

Finish stuff the same day and have an easy morning:

If possible get to the finish line on as many jobs as possible the same day — even if it means staying back a little. This not only gives you the satisfaction of having 'accomplished' things but also leaves you with a less crowded morning the next day. Usually, mornings are the most hectic when the whole world seems to crash on your head, so if have an easy first half you'll feel blessed.

Have an overnight list:

Let's say you couldn't finish everything by evening. No sweat, make a small list of the remaining jobs and carry it with you. Paste it on the washroom mirror – it will help keep you focused. You'll see the list again in the morning as you get ready, giving you a snapshot of work that needs immediate attention. Also, you'll get the chance to review them mentally, and you can launch into completing them as soon as you reach office.

Time management is the single most important habit of successful entrepreneurs and that the rest of us need to emulate it. They know that punctuality is not just about coming to work on time or reaching appointments on the dot. It is also about meeting work timelines, every single time. That requires practice, and the patience to understand how time works for you – and how you respond to its demands. You must get on top of punctuality because that's an important quality in you that tells your employer that you are money well spent.

It is a skill you need to master like any skill; it needs learning a few things and unlearning a few others. Above all, it requires your application – and appreciation that chronic lateness can be a problem that requires focused attention. It needs your single-minded commitment to attack it, and come to a satisfactory set of solutions. Keep reading and we'll feed you more methods to do just that.

Punctuality Punch

What's worse than running late for an appointment? Not letting the other party know about it. In today's times of cell phones and tablets, the easiest thing is to let people know how late you are likely to be. It indicates that you treat the client with respect and that you value their time, but let your reason be genuine. For example, if you are stuck in traffic, it is a helpless situation. So the least you can do is inform your client that way they can get something else done in the meantime. It is the polite things to do, and it helps you forge a better relationship with your client.

TRY THIS TODAY!

Listen to the radio in the mornings. Most stations (or radio jockeys) keep announcing the time every now and then, so you can be on your toes without physically checking the clock.

Chapter 4: How To Make A Good To-Do List

It's relatively easy to make a good to-do list. Anybody who knows how to read and write can do it. Making a good one however is an entirely different thing.

In making your to-do list, it's important to remember why are you doing it. The single best reason to do it is because you want to optimize personal productivity by becoming more efficient in terms of managing your tasks, which requires both focus and organization. By efficiently organizing the things you need to do, you'll be able to focus better on the things that truly matter.

Only tasks

When you list down the items for inclusion in your to-do list, you must know how to tell the difference between tasks, goals and projects. Your to-do lists should only contain tasks and not projects or goals. When you mix together tasks and projects in your to-do lists, you may get confused.

By limiting the items to tasks only, you'll be able to better organize and focus only on things that really matter.

Take for example your spouse or any loved one. Say you want to make him or her feel appreciated and loved on their birthday, which is just around the corner. Is that a task or a goal? That's right, it's a goal that you want to achieve. Now, how do you plan to achieve that goal? Maybe you'd like to surprise him or her with a party at home, which is a project. And what are the actionable steps required to complete the project? These would include canvassing for a venue, choosing what foods to serve, cooking the food, printing the invitations, sending the invitations and preparing activities for the party, among other things.

Imagine if you can how it'd look like if you include projects and goals in your to do lists. If you can't, it'd probably look like this:

-Throw surprise party;

-Choose food to serve;

-Make spouse or loved one feel appreciated and loved;

-Send invitations;

-Print invitations;

-Canvass venue; and

-Prepare activities for the party.

Doesn't it look rather confusing? Further, doesn't it run the risk of doing some things twice? Now that's what I'm talking about.

Smaller tasks

Good to-do lists are those that can be managed well. The best way to make them as such is by breaking down tasks that are complicated and big into much smaller ones. To the extent possible, include only those tasks that can be done in one sitting and by you alone. Let's go back to the surprise party example, shall we?

Let's take the task "prepare activities for the party". You can actually break this down further into even smaller tasks and ask help from other people such as:

-Researching popular party games;

-Buying materials for activities; and

-Facilitate activities.

As you can see, these smaller tasks can be done in one step or by you alone. As such, it makes your to-do list – at least for the surprise party – much simpler and clearer.

Labels

Now that you've broken down your tasks into simplest and most basic level, you must label them as much as possible with the necessary info. It makes your to-do lists even clearer and easier to manage.

Let's refer to the surprise party example again. Let's say you've limited the number of activities you'd like to conduct for the party to just 5. You can label each of those 5 choices with information like "props intensive", "little to no props needed" and "children's games" or "adults' games" so you don't have to look further into their details in order to quickly categorize them and schedule them in the program. It may not seem much but when you're doing a lot of things, even the few seconds saved counts.

Priorities

The final characteristic of good to-do lists is priorities. Each task is different and as such, they're also not equal in importance or urgency. A good way of prioritizing our tasks is by using the late Stephen Covey's quadrants that was popularized in his classic best-selling book How to Win Friends and Influence People. These quadrants are:

-I: Important and urgent tasks;

-II: Important but not urgent tasks;

-III: Un-important but urgent tasks; and

-IV: Un-important and not urgent tasks.

Obviously, top priority should be given to Quadrant I tasks, such as bringing your child to the doctor after having on and off fever for 3 days now and paying your overdue credit card bills. Both tasks aren't just important but need to be acted on now.

Second priority must be reserved for Quadrant II tasks because even if they're not urgent, they're important and neglecting them can have dire consequences. Examples of these would be bringing your car to the shop for periodic maintenance works like tune ups and change oils and regular exercise. Putting them off until they become urgent may already be too late and in these examples, may already cause irreparable damage to your car and health, respectively.

Tasks under Quadrant III should be given very little, if any, priority because while they may be urgent, they're not important. Not accomplishing these tasks only has minor repercussions, if at all. These include tasks like picking up a ringing telephone.

Lastly, no priority should be given to Quadrant IV activities because they're both unimportant and not urgent. Why waste your precious time on them right? Life's too short to waste time and energy on such tasks.

This is a very important aspect of your TDL that you shouldn't take for granted for herein lies the secret to focusing for greater personal efficiency and productivity. By focusing on the big-ticket items first, you accomplish more for the same, if not less, time and other resources.

Alternative: The Action Plan

Making a to-do list is basic among everyone from the wingers to the obsessive-compulsive. We have discussed at length at how to make a to-do list, but here are some tips to make sure the to-do list sticks. An action plan that makes you want to get up and actually do it!

• Pick a medium.

To-do lists come in all shapes and sizes, so it's all about what works for the individual. Maybe writing the tasks down on pen and paper is one of those ways. If so, you can also use digital apps to help make such to-do lists.

• Make multiple lists

It never hurts to be prepared and have a back-up. For the most part, a master list with all the long-term goals like cleaning the garage or finishing a due assignment a month from should be kept. There should also be a weekly project list; self-explanatory. Finally, on the most important lists to keep around should be the HIT list, or high-impact task. That should include stuff needed to be done today like walking the dogs or picking up the dry cleaning. The HIT list will never run out of tasks because some of them are required to be done daily, such as dog walking. Also, tasks on the master list and weekly list may pop up on HIT sooner or later.

- KISS

The acronym for Keep It Simple, Stupid. And nothing's more simple then avoiding to intimidate yourself scared and silly with a very long to-do list. You know, so long that it's unreasonable to get it all done in 24 hours. A trick to having a simple HIT list is to put all the stuff you want to do that day and then cut it in half. There should be 10 tasks or less on there, and what isn't mandatory can go toward your weekly or master list.

- MIT

Another acronym, standing for Most Important Tasks. Start the list with at two or more items that absolutely must get done today, so you don't end up vacuuming instead of finishing a project report due tomorrow. Even if the rest of the list stays untouched, the really meaningful stuff will get finished.

• Start easy.

Be sure to stick a few simple items on the MIT list. Some good examples include "fold clothes," "wash breakfast dishes," and "shower". You can even cross off silly stuff to help start the day feeling super-productive.

• Break it down.

Goals such as "work on research paper" are much too vague and intimidating, meaning we'll be too afraid to actually start tackling them. You can reduce the fear and make your goals seem more manageable if you break projects down into smaller tasks. So instead of an open goal like the original "work on research paper", go for something specific like "write first half of chapter three" for Monday, and "finish second half" on Tuesday.

• Stay specific.

If there's anything to-do lists have in common, it's they have the qualities of physical actions. Meaning, they can be finished in one sitting, and they're the tasks only the to-do-list writer can do. For general projects that require a lot of time or some extra help, be specific about what to do for those steps to the main goal. Something like "write a cover letter for internship at World Wildlife Fund" sounds more specific and professional than just "save the animals"

• Include it all.

For every task on the list, be sure to add as much information as possible so you can get the job done. Like if the task needs you to call someone, add their phone number on the list to save time and effort looking for it later.

• Time it.

Now that you've made the list (and checked it twice), go back and put a time estimate next to every item. It might even help to turn the to-do list into a kind of schedule with specific times and places. For example: laundry 4-6 p.m. at Suds & Stuff, clean out inbox 6-7 p.m. at Starbucks on 6th Ave. When time's up, it's up; there's no spending six hours at the Laundromat.

• Don't stress.

Every master list has a few tasks that you want to do for days, weeks, and maybe years, but haven't gotten around to. Try to figure out why you haven't done so in order to make the necessary steps to actually complete the task, or tasks. If you don't want to "Call Uncle Pat" because of fear of getting stuck talking with him all day, then "Figure out a way to get off the phone with Uncle Pat." The big task will seem easier and get done faster.

• Make it public.

Sometimes the best way to stay accountable is to have someone watch over us. So, share that to-do list with someone by sticking it on a refrigerator magnet or setting up a digital calendar for the work team to see and access.

• Schedule scheduling.

A tricky aspect to the to-do list is actually sitting down to make one. Pick a time every day to get yourself organized and get stuff done. Breakfast, lunch, dinner, crazy late hours while everyone else is asleep, just make sure it works for you.

• Go in with the old.

A way to boost productivity is to remind yourself how productive you were yesterday. A written list of everything that has been done the day before, even small stuff, can help convince you that you earned a pat on the back and can keep going.

• Start fresh.

Make a new list every day so the old items don't clog up the agenda or get forgotten. This is useful to make sure you have something done daily and don't just waste time decorating the paper with highlighter marks.

• Be flexible.

Here's a tip: always leave within 15 minutes of "cushion time" when making your scheduled to-do list or calendar. Something may pop-up that throws off your tight schedule, like a flooding bathroom or a computer crash. The most important thing is to keep calm and carry on with deep breaths. Hopefully you can get a few MITs done beforehand too.

Chapter 5: Why Are You Procrastinating?

Each of us have different reasons for procrastinating and in this chapter, we are going to find out what is motivating you to procrastinate. You see, as humans, we never do something unless we are receiving some type of benefit out of it. One of the main reasons people procrastinate is because the task seems as if it will be dull or boring. Often times we think something is going to take a long time and it is going to be boring to do, we set ourselves up for failure by doing this.

7. Change your mindset. If you start a task thinking it is going to be boring or it is going to drag on and on, that is exactly what is going to happen. You need to change the way you think about the task you need to complete. Think about it like this, when I have a specific job that I know I am going to enjoy doing, it does not take any amount of pushing to get myself to start the job. I complete the job quickly because I knew I would enjoy it. Now

when I used to have jobs that sounded completely boring to me, I would put it off and then when I finally started it I would allow myself to get distracted. Now I know I need to start the job as soon as possible and just get it done. I know the sooner I get it done, the better I am going to feel and I will not have to deal with a sense of dread when it comes to that job. It was all about changing how I thought about the work.

The next reason people tend to procrastinate is because they are not organized or they forget that they are supposed to complete a specific task. This is another reason that keeping a notebook is so very important. If you find that you are just aimlessly wondering and have nothing to do, you can quickly refer to your notebook and remind yourself of what needs to be done. This is very important if you are working from home. Often times you will accept work and then even though you know it needs to be done, you will busy yourself with other tasks. The next thing you know your client is asking why you have not completed the job. You absolutely have to write everything down that you need to complete so that you are not forgetting anything. You cannot expect to remember to do everything you are supposed to on any given day.

People so tend to procrastinate because they are insecure, suffer from self-doubt or even fear of failure. This is where you are going to have to do a bit of work on yourself.

8. Understand where the self-d0ubt or fear of failure comes from. Often times it comes from a series of experiences we had when we were younger. No one ever suddenly begins to doubt themselves when they try to complete a task. It could be rooted in some failure that happened to you at some point in your life where others acted as if they were disappointed in you. Once you understand where the self-doubt comes from, you will be able to use it to your advantage.

I suffered with self-doubt my entire life because I was raised in a family where I was told I was weak or I couldn't do certain. I began to believe that I was weak, but let me tell you when you are starting a business from home, you don't have time to be weak or allow your fears to direct your actions. This is just what worked for me and it may work for you as well. I took all of that doubt that I knew had nothing to do with who I really was as a person, and used it to fuel myself. I was going to prove everyone who said I could not make it on my own wrong. I was going to show them that I no longer was weak.

When you start a task you need to tell yourself that you can do it. You see, when you tell yourself you can't do something you are going to do whatever needs to be done to prove yourself right. The same thing is true if you tell yourself you can do something. If you feel like you are unable to overcome the self-doubt you are dealing with, you may want to consider some form of counseling.

9. Use positive affirmations to help you complete the tasks you need to do. If one thing has changed my life, it is the use of

positive affirmations, believing that I was able to accomplish all that I needed to accomplish. I started replacing all of my negative thoughts with positive ones. I suggest that you at least give them a try. You can find tons of recordings online for free and if you try them for a few weeks I am sure you will see a huge difference as well.

The final reason I want to talk about in this chapter is impulsiveness, indecisiveness or immaturity. I am a very impulsive person, I also have a ton of hobbies. If I was working online and happened to come across something that interested me or had something to do with one of my hobbies, I would push my work to the side and focus on the hobby. For example, I am one of those people who look for great deals and use coupons to get free stuff. So if I happened to come across a deal while I was online I would completely forget what I was doing, grab my coupons and head out the door. I suppose this had a lot to do with immaturity as well. Although I view couponing as a very important part of my life, it is a way I save tons of money for my family, it is not the most important thing I needed to be doing.

I could have simply as I do now written the deal down, went on with my work and went and bought the items after I finished my job. This is where we all have to learn to grow up and it is extremely important if you are working from home.

10. Keep a list of priorities and consider how your actions are affecting those priorities. In the back of my schedule notebook I have a list of my priorities, when I feel tempted to procrastinate and move off of the task at hand, I simply flip to the back of my notebook and ask myself if that decision will benefit the things that are the most important to me. Take the couponing for example. I ask myself if doing that task is going to benefit my family? The answer is yes. Is it going to save me money? The answer is yes. Is it going to benefit my business? The answer is no! Then I have to ask myself if the task can be done later and of course the answer is yes. After you start breaking

things down like this on a regular basis, you will naturally start thinking this way whenever you have any decision to make.

Chapter 6: Utilizing Your Time To Achieve Effectiveness

In the previous chapter, you've learned about the importance of delegation. In this chapter, we're going to talk about two parts. First, is the art of delegating; and second, right after delegation, an answer to the question: how do you spend your time? Let's get started.

STEPS FOR EFFECTIVE DELEGATION

Be empowered. If you feel that you're not empowered enough to make decisions involving the task at hand, you might end up doing three things: going back to your superiors to ask for help, delaying work, or reversing the delegation process. The first two can happen but they can be fixed. But the third one is a challenge. Why?

Reversing the delegation process means that the task you have previously delegated ends up coming back to you for completion. Why does this happen? When you don't provide all of the pre-requisites to complete a task, like clear instructions, accountability and commitment statements, training or resources, and proper coaching and monitoring, you might be forced to take back the task.

As the delegator, this shouldn't happen. If your team member makes a mistake, let him or her take that as a learning opportunity and help him or her get a fresh start.

Prepare the task specifications. From the moment you delegate the task up to when it gets completed, you must have a plan. Be clear about your expectations and the kind of results you want to get, including the person who you want to get it done. A well-thought plan prevents you from switching expectations. And mind you, if that happens, the person doing it may get confused and may waste time complaining rather than doing.

Provide context. Start by explaining why you're delegating that specific task to your team member. When you provide context, do it in a way that your team member understands that this task can help them grow and can prepare them for more responsibilities in the future. If they clearly see how accepting this task can provide them with value (and how it can lend credence to their resume), they'll have no qualms about getting it done.

Officially assign. Once your team member understands the context of the assignment, you can then provide him or her with clear execution guidelines. Take note that these guidelines does not involve the specific of the tasks. At this point, your focus is on deliverability. So discuss timing, budget if applicable, frequency of communication and update, and reporting structure.

Give clear instructions. This step is now more task-specific. Whether a task is short or long-term, you need to be able to communicate the different phases that your team member needs to complete. If a task is complicated, divide it into executable parts matched with realistic timelines. Also be aware of dependencies. Bit by bit, explain to them what they need to accomplish by doing one sub-task after another.

Confirm understanding. Before setting off to work, you need to make sure that your team member understands what needs to be accomplished and how to get it accomplished. If asking your team member to paraphrase the things you've said makes you uncomfortable, ask questions. Commonly, it only takes a minute to confirm understanding but then if there are blurred lines that are unclarified, you might end up not achieving the goal.

Ask for commitment. And don't simply ask for it. Confirm it. Make sure that your team member fully understands the role that this task plays in reference to the big goals you want to achieve. Also ensure that he or she understands the consequences of not being able to deliver the expected results.

Delegate accountability. In view of commitment, make sure that your team member knows that he or she is accountable for not meeting deadlines, quality results, etc. The key to monitoring his or her progress? Constant communication. An update submitted once a week would be nice. It's entirely up to you and the nature of the task.

Provide training and resources. If needed, train your team member so he or she can perform the task more effectively. Note that it's your duty to make sure that your team member possesses the skills, knowledge, and resources needed in order to be able to fulfill the requirements of his or her job.

Celebrate milestones. No, you don't have to go out for lunch or dinner each time you reach a milestone. Instead, recognize the victories that your team member has accomplished. He or she deserves it. And on top of that, when the task is done, don't forget to express gratitude. A simple 'Thank You' can help your team member realize that he or she has done something to positively contribute to your team. And take note, these simple moments are actually remembered.

Undoubtedly, the process of delegation outlined in the steps above constitutes one of your activities as an effective manager. That brings us to the next topic in this chapter which involves answering the question, 'How do you spend your time?'

HOW DO YOU SPEND YOUR TIME?

It's easier to answer this question if you relate it to the process of budgeting. Yes, that part when you go through figuring out how much you've spent and how much you've saved in a month. And just like money, you need a quantifiable element in order to track how you're spending your time. In this case, that's it in itself: time.

There are three ways at which you can track your time spending. First, you can use time-tracking applications. There are tons of them online with the free ones offering you enough features to implement a time management plan. Second, if you're working on predetermined hours per task, you can monitor the length of time it took you to complete each task. And third, if you're working the 9-5 round, you can manually log your activities in a spreadsheet.

Regardless of how you decide to track time, you need to be aware of three things. First, the amount of time you've spent finishing off each task on your list. Second, how many tasks you were able to complete and how much free time you have left. This can be your total time or aggregated time. And third, what you have done during your entire time.

Now, if you maintain a record of the things mentioned above, you'll discover things as you'll do when looking at your spending pattern. Which activities were actually relevant? How long have you spent on each of them? Which activities are irrelevant? How did they affect your supposedly productive hours? What do you plan to do about them?

Ponder on these questions and make a plan of action. You can't be spending too much time on something that you're not supposed to.

THE SMART SCHEDULER: SETTING YOUR PRIORITIES

Have you ever felt like being unaccomplished despite having arrived at work early and having left so late? Once in a while, this feeling is acceptable. But if you feel it too often, you might not be working out your day-to-day priorities pretty well. This article focuses on how you can set your priorities well and be a champion of your own schedule. But first, let's take a look at the not-so-obvious importance of having a schedule.

WHY HAVING A SCHEDULE IS ESSENTIAL

Being realistic about what you can achieve with the time you have. You might be one of those people who continuously wish to have a 36-hour daytime. Tough luck. Perhaps the reason why you only have 24 hours in a day is for you to have time to actually identify your priorities. When you know what your priorities are, you're bound to stay realistic. Tomorrow is another day.

Schedules help you stick to the essentials tasks. But what can you call 'essential tasks?' A smart definition would be the tasks that can help you achieve your goal – goal for the day, goal for the week; short-term goals or long-term goals. By having a schedule, you'll know if you need to cut some time doing the non-essentials.

Being realistically hardworking. How much can you take? How do you know if you're taking too much of what you can handle? The answer lies on your schedule. And know that a schedule so full doesn't equate to being busy. It doesn't even equate to being productive or effective. A full schedule only tells you that you might be working yourself too hard that by the time you realize it, you're nearly burning out.

Work-life balance. In an ever-busy era, you might have heard some people stake a bold claim: work-life balance isn't real anymore. Whether or not you believe that, it pays to reconsider your position. What can you do? Check your calendar. When was the last time you actually left work on time? When was the last time you didn't purposively go to work way too early? When was the last time you actually thought that the issue might be on your time management capability?

Time for yourself, your family, your family, and the world. As society becomes more and more industrialized, we become more connected to each other. The idea that a small boxed object called a smartphone can actually be used to talk to someone on the other side of the world is nothing short of a miracle. But this just proves that no one really lives under a rock now. And no one can actually spend the rest of his or her life being disconnected from the world. Check your schedule. Have you really no time to go out and to have fun?

Now: how to schedule your time and how to identify your priorities.

HOW TO SCHEDULE YOUR TIME AND PRIORITIZE

Let it be known that when you learn how to effectively schedule your time, you can also minimize your stress levels. Why so? Because organization comes into play. You'll minimize being the buzzer beater, and you won't cause stress to the people around you – especially those who are waiting on you. These five tips are simple but when you practice it faithfully, you can own your time.

Have a regular scheduling time. Scheduling your time requires time as well. It involves planning so you need to be set to do it. Otherwise, you might not be planning your schedule based on your essential tasks. Some people find it helpful to schedule their time on weekly basis. Some find it more beneficial to do monthly planning. Regardless, if you have a fair idea of how your week or month will progress, you have a better chance of getting a locked schedule.

Find your available times. Your available time is the time when you're willing to work. In industries where hours are allocated instead of consumed, this is very useful. If you're on a fixed-hour schedule, you can also benefit from properly mapping out your time so that you know how much free time you have left.

Note that allocating or consuming your hours is also dependent on the nature of your job and your professional and personal goals. If you're eyeing to have more time to do non-work-related tasks, you might plan your available time based on the amount of task you're required to complete.

Schedule essential tasks within your available times. This is now entirely dependent on the primary metrics that your job title, scope, or responsibility requires. These are the tasks that you're being assessed against, and the tasks that tell your superiors that you're doing a great job.

So now you understand that essentials tasks are non-negotiable. These are expected of you and from you. If you're a Social Media Manager, for example, a part of what constitutes your essentials tasks would be planning the monthly editorial calendar or making sure that a post goes live based on the frequency that you set to your client.

Distinguish between essential, priority, and urgent tasks. To put simply, essential tasks are those that you can't relegate, defer, or avoid. Priority tasks are those that you need to complete during the day before you can move on to your other tasks. Urgent tasks are time-bound and need to be completed within the timeline specified.

All three types of tasks are dependent on each other because they share something in common: they're tied to a goal. So, recognize that while you're planning to make sure you constantly deliver what's expected from you, you also need to plan so that you can accurately respond to pressing matters that are unexpected.

Discover your discretionary time. Discretionary time is the time you have left after factoring in your essential tasks, priority tasks, and urgent tasks. Because it's discretionary, you can use it in your own volition.

Now, one important thing that you need to remember is that as long as you're at work, or as long as you're fulfilling your planned time allocation, discretionary time shouldn't be spent for personal endeavors. A good way to make use of discretionary time is to review your goals within the company, get ahead of other upcoming tasks, or spend some time meeting with the members of your team.

Finally, what good is a schedule if you don't analyze its effectiveness? Considering that you have entered items in your schedule under the three types of tasks discussed, it's also worth analyzing if these tasks are something that you can delegate, outsource, or automate.

Chapter 7: How To Hack Your Brain (And Life) For Maximum Time-Management Awesomeness

"The bad news is time flies. The good news is, you're the pilot."

-Michael Altahuler

This is where MOST "Time Management" books start things off by talking about priorities. About the need to have a clear idea of what EXACTLY you're trying to accomplish. (And figure out a plan for making it happen.)

And the whole trick to "time management" — they'll tout — is to ensure a majority of your energy each day is spent on activities that move you closer to these objectives and goals. (And then they spend 300 more pages reiterating this fact. Usually with graphs.)

And, you know what, they're right. It's vital you don't waste precious time on non-essential crap. (Unless you consider binge-watching Stranger Things essential.)

And we're gonna cover all that prioritization stuff in the next chapter. Promise.

But in my experience, it's better to set priorities and create those beautiful 5-year objective plans — complete with poster board and colored markers — after you've looked at how you handle time NOW. (And implement quick-fix solutions to get you more productive right away, not 300 pages later.)

Because all the white-board planning and Mind Map documents won't do any good if, deep down, you don't know how you're currently sabotaging your time. (And trust me, you are. Even if you don't know it.)

Best part is: after doing the strategies I'm about to encourage you do for the next week, you'll have a CLEAR picture of how you spend your time — which will give you the foundation you need to make quick, effective changes to your productivity.

So, don't worry. In the next couple chapters, we're gonna go all office-supply crazy and get you a calendar/planner system that will make your economics teacher from high school proud.

But for now, let's dip our toe into the "Time Management" waters with my "5 Keys to Hacking Your Brain for Time-Management Awesomeness:"

Brain Hack #1: Track How You Spend Your Time

I know. You've heard this time-management nugget before. ("Keep track of how you spend your time, down to the minute, so you slowly go insane.")

And while I'm sure you understand the importance of knowing how spend your time, you'd rather watch Justin Bieber play Hamlet on Broadway than track every minute of your day. ("To be or not to be, girl, that's what I'm sayin...")

Here are a couple of things to keep in mind about "time-tracking" (as the over-priced experts call it):

1.   You don't have to track time for the rest of your life. Just a week. Though you might get addicted to it. (I did.)

2.   You don't have to track EVERY minute. Just track in fifteen- or thirty-minute — even sixty-minute — chunks. Whatever you can do.

3.   Time-tracking is not about making you feel bad. There are plenty of other tools for that. Facebook . Phone calls with your mother. The look your wife gives you when you tell her you quit your job to play video games professionally. Time-tracking is about finding out how you spend your time. (Usually different from how you think.)

4.   You'll find you do more fun stuff than you think you do. I know you "think" you spend 12 hours a day chained to your laptop. But by doing this exercise you'll find you DO get in more fun, diversionary activities than you think you do.

5.   It's okay if you MISS a couple time chunks. You aren't sitting for the Bar exam. Do the best you can.

6.   You will, without noticing, become more conscious of how you spend time. This is what makes time-tracking so

addicting. You'll get this subtle (but powerful) awareness of what the frick you do all day long. And you'll be better equipped to make conscious decisions about what you WANT to do. (Instead of getting caught up in binge-watching Season 3 of Columbo. Which is not the worst thing in the world.)

Now, as for the actual time-tracking "tech," you have many choices. (Some decent.) Here are a couple of my faves:

• Good, old pen and paper - I started off using this. And if it weren't for the fact that my handwriting is just slightly more legible than a three-year-old's, I'd still be using it. (Pros: Cheap, easy. Cons: Not super portable, a pain to track in bulk.)

• Excel (or Google) spreadsheet - This is the method I moved to after pen-and-paper and still use from time-to-time. (I'm old-fashioned and resistant to change.) What I like about word-processing spreadsheets is I'm forced to input the data; this forces me to...you know...think about the intel. (Pros: Portable, Easy to use. Cons: Not automated (you gotta input the info); Compatibility can be an issue.)

• Toggl - Probably the most powerful (and affordable) time-tracking app out there. (Namely because it's FREE!) A great tool if you have a team of employees — you can create sub-projects, reports and even friendly productivity competitions — or if you're a freelancer trying to keep track of your day. (Pros: Free, until you get more than five team members; versatile features for teams. Cons: Slight learning curve.)

• Fresh Books - If you're a freelancer, who bills hours to numerous clients — and need detailed reporting — this is your best bet. Just hit "time" on your app and it'll automatically keep track of which project (or client) your time is apportioned to. (Pros: Great for freelancers; Automated; Integrates with Google and Stripe. Cons: Gets expensive if more than 25 clients; Overkill for solo-preneurs.)

Brain Hack #2: Create Your Daily Three

So, in the next chapter we're gonna go over setting priorities and creating a daily, weekly, and yearly schedule that helps you achieve your objectives. But for now, I'd like you to "start" implementing one daily prioritization strategy.

And that's the "Daily Three."

It works like this: each morning (or night before) write down THREE THINGS you've gotta get done that day. (And would make you feel like a moronic failure if you weren't able to execute.)

These shouldn't be huge, epic tasks. Like "Write my novel." Or easy tasks like "Compose a tweet."

They should be moderately-significant activities that take about 30-60 minutes a piece. And they should contribute DIRECTLY to the bottom-line of your day-to-day entrepreneurial life. (Not just stuff you want to cross off your to-do list.)

Updating your company's Facebook page or churning out content for your Twitter account may prove interesting to your 12 followers — and might give you the satisfaction you aren't alone in a cold universe — but they don't belong in your "Daily Three."

And here's the magical part: The goal of the "Daily Three" is to get all three done before LUNCH.

What? What blasphemy is this that I speak?

That's right! Your task, if you choose to accept it, each day is to do your damnedest to knock off each of the "Daily Three" before you head to the kitchen and heat up that day-old slice of Pepperoni & Mushroom Pizza...I mean, prepare a bowl of organic quinoa and kale soup.

Of course, this isn't always possible. Life happens. Things come up.

You gotta take the dog to the vet. Or you get an emergency customer service call from that loony client in a psychotic break.

Which is why it's a game. You're trying to cheat-code the system and get around the laws of traditional work physics and get a helluva lot more done than anybody else, including you, thought possible. ("We do more before 10 a.m...blah, blah, blah...")

Because here's the monumentally cool thing: If you're able to get even TWO of the "Daily Three" done by noon you'll feel such a sense of accomplishment — and total kick-ass momentum — that doing the third task will be a breeze. And free you up for other areas of your life that need addressing. (Such as those super-fun activities we'll go over in Chapter 2.)

For now, just pick out your "Daily Three" and gamify your efforts toward getting 'em all done before you press "Start" on the microwave.

Brain Hack #3: Learn to Work in Timed, Laser-Focused Bursts of Awesomeness

This might be the most life-changing strategy in the entire book. Because this one strategy alone has increased my productivity at least 300%. (And doesn't require a single six-pack of Diet Mountain Dew.)

And that is to structure your work sessions in timed, focused segments in which you work on ONE THING and one thing only.

Sounds simple. I know you and I both "think" we're optimized machines of focused, productive work.

But the truth is more humbling:

•   The average worker checks their email 30 times an hour

•   The average worker checks their smartphone 150 times a day

•   The average worker's length of uninterrupted focus is eight minutes

Of course, you and I are FAR from average. (You're reading this book, after all.)

But how many times have you sat down to work and suddenly your smartphone pops up with a notification? Or during a work session you suddenly feel the urge to check ESPN to see if your beloved San Diego Padres beat the Giants? (They didn't. Don't worry.)

This is what, in the $500/hr productivity consultant biz, they call "switch tasking." (The term "Multi-tasking" isn't used much these days; it's impossible to work on two things at once, turns out.)

And the mental cost of "switch tasking" is severe. Not only in wasted time but in the amount of mental energy required to get back on track. (This is how you can spend eight hours staring at your computer, be totally exhausted, and get nothing done.)

The solution is, instead, to work in focused bursts of time. (With intermittent breaks in between.) Now there are many ways to approach this form of focused work. But I like the Pomodoro Method, invented by the developer Francesco Cirillo.

The method works like this:

• Work for 25 minutes on one task

• Take a break for 5 minutes

• Repeat this routine of 25-minute blocks (and 5-minute breaks) three more times.

• After you've finished 4 25-minute blocks, take an extended break of 30-60 minutes.

• Rinse and repeat

You don't have to be a control-freak about these sessions. I tend to work past the 25-minute mark when I'm cooking and give myself a longer-than-five-minute break when I'm finished.

The key is to train your mind to work on one thing, for a specific period. (And nothing else!)

There are a ton of digital Pomodoro timer apps options out there, and some physical ones as well. I like "Tomato Timer" for the desktop and Simple Pomodoro for the tablet. (I try not to use my smartphone as a timing device; I've weened myself off smartphone notifications. (But that's just cos I have ZERO attention span.)

If you'd like a complete walk-through on the Pomodoro technique, check out this cool column over at Lifehacker: DriveThruMBA.com/Pomodoro.

But ease into these 25-minute blocks. Start with 10, maybe 15 minutes of focused, one-task work. And work your way up until your schedule is chock-full of 25-minute blocks of awesomeness. (You'll find you get more done in far less time.)

Brain Hack #4: Assess Your Data (and Make a Daily "Win Tally')

Once you've started "time-tracking," it's a good idea to examine the intel you've collected. (Even after just one day.)

But instead of using it as an excuse to brand yourself as the "laziest human being on the face of the Earth" — sorry, I've got that title wrapped up — you want to use it to:

• Figure out what you're getting done daily

• Make positive changes to your productivity routine

• Create a "win tally" that collects kick-ass things you did each day

It's that last one where I veer off from the rest of the time-management gurus. Yes, it's good to use "time-tracking" to gain insight into how you can boost productivity.

But it's also an easy way to boost feelings of satisfaction and self-confidence. Which, in turn, lead to sustained, long-term productivity.

So, here's what I recommend you do at the end of each workday. Pull out your time-tracking sheet, along with a small notepad and:

1.   Circle (or bold) periods of focused work activity. The good stuff.

2.   Italicize or (star) any BIG gaps in productivity. Anything more than 15 minutes.

3.   Looking at your gaps ask yourself: Is there anything I could have done to reduce those gaps? Could you have brought a notepad with you to work while waiting in the doctor's office? Or maybe NOT turn on the TV after lunch and watch three episodes of The Rockford Files?

4.   Write down ideas you have for improving workflow. Don't focus on generalized personality traits, like "Not be a lazy SOB." Instead look for constructive actions you can take, such as "moving high-priority stuff to before lunch" or

"scheduling less than three meetings a day."

5.   Write down three "wins" you had each day. Wins can be almost anything: "The fact you finally wrote the opening chapter to your non-fiction how-to book." Or that you "got enough stuff done to watch your kid play an afternoon Little League game." Or maybe that "you're compiling a 'daily win tally' right this moment." That counts!

I know that last strategy may seem a bit new-agey for your tastes — it did for me when I started. But there's something powerful about recognizing awesome things you did over the course of a day. (All while striving to improve your overall day-to-day productivity.)

Who knows? You might end up becoming so productive — and wealthy — you end up buying your own Major League Baseball team. (Here's hoping they beat the Giants more than my Padres.)

Chapter's Action Steps

• Use "time-tracking" to see how you spend your time. Use whatever form you like — digital, paper, excel sheet, stone tablet — just make sure to use it as information — not an excuse to hate yourself.

• Commit to starting each workday by coming up with a "Daily Three" — three items you'd feel like an idiot if you didn't accomplish that day. Then do your best to get 'em all done before lunch. (Gamify it!)

• Train your brain to work in focused, timed segments. The author likes the Pomodoro method — 25 minutes of work, followed by five minutes of checking ESPN scores. But whatever you do, work on one thing, and one thing only, during that 25-minute block.

• Do a quick review of your "time-tracking" each day. Highlight big gaps and areas of focused work. Brainstorm ways you could have improved your productivity — and don't forget to tally them wins!

Chapter 8: Quick Hacks To Help Daily Schedules

All these things I have mentioned are those habits you have to make part of your daily routine in order to make sure you have a proper balance between your work and your personal lives. You have to take the time to internalize them and make them second nature – and it is not an easy task. Keep at it, do not give up and you will find that, soon enough, you've learnt how to manage your time properly!

Other than these routine changes, here are some very specific, very quick hacks you can follow to help you manage your schedule for the day –

Use your car-time to be productive

If you are stuck in traffic, don't panic. Instead take that time to mentally sort through all that you have to do for the day, and make a quick to-do list at the back of your mind. You can even keep a pen and some sticky-notes that you can stick to the dashboard to help you remember! For those of you, who are not comfortable with working this way, use your car-time to relax instead of getting agitated at the traffic! Listen to music, maybe, or sing along so that your spirits are up when you reach your place of work.

Instead of pushing yourself even harder or sacrificing more time for your career, why don't you consider using your daily transportation time as an opportunity to get more work done during the day. Most people on average drive at least 30 minutes one way just to get to their offices or their businesses. This means a significant amount of time is normally available for more productive uses. While it's quite obvious that it is not a good idea to drive and work at the same time, you can consider commuting daily so you can have more time for more productive activities. Here are some ways you can use your daily commuting time to be more productive.

Listen

Whether you ride the bus or a carpool to work or to school, you can use your commuting time to be updated on the latest news or even get a high level overview of a particular video lesson have just watched. Most of these lessons, also called webinars, give free downloads of the sessions afterwards. After downloading them, you can just as easily take away the audio part for further listening at your own convenient time. You can also try downloading audio versions of books and while on your daily commute, you can listen to these materials. In particular, listen to those that are relevant to your career, your job, or whatever it is your studying in school.

The only drawback to this particular way of maximizing your commuting time is that you really don't have any chances to take notes. But if the material you're trying to listen to is not the top priority, then you could simply make extra time for reading and notes taking later on.

Telecommunicate

You can also catch up on your communication duties by holding teleconferences or debriefings while on your daily commute. This will be however, depends on the type of transportation you are going to ride. As you well know, meetings can usually take at least half an hour or more and would involve at least several of your subordinates, which could grading stuff for productivity. If you're driving and you're comfortable using a hands-free set with your phone, you can hold a meeting while you're on your way to work. This can be particularly useful if you normally have your meetings either first thing in the morning or right before you leave your office or business. While it's true that nothing beats face-to-face meetings, there are meetings that you can afford to conduct through telecommunication. So while you're on your way to work or from it, why not make the most out of it?

Another productive thing that you can do while commuting is to catch up on all of your pending voicemail. Effective and productive communication isn't limited to just face to face meetings. Again, if you have access to a hands-free set for your cellular phone and you are either commuting or driving to and from work, you can easily review your pending voicemails without having to take away time from work. As such, can also use of time to make those necessary return calls you have been putting off since yesterday. To the extent that you can pull this strategy off efficiently, it's also the extent by which you can experience more flexibility and productivity by being able to take and make phone calls at your discretion or most convenient time.

Carpooling

While this is certainly not for everyone, this is a very good option he happen to live within proximity to all your other coworkers or classmates. All of you can save much time and energy simply by going to and from work or class together in one car. Say there are four of you carpooling together. Each of you can alternate in terms of driving responsibilities once or twice a week, depending on the rotation. That effectively frees up at least 3 days for each one in terms of driving responsibilities. These three days can then be used to get extra work done while enjoying the ride. On average, this would mean about two to three hours of extra time for work or study every week. You also get to save on gasoline expenses too.

Carpooling offers another opportunity to increase productivity, particularly if all your carpool mates happened to be your classmates or your office mates. Your daily commute can then be an opportunity to discuss and read about important things face to face without having to commit yourselves to actual meetings at the office or in school, especially during your busiest hours.

Techno-Commute

You can also use technology to your advantage to be more productive during your daily commuting time. You can either bring your laptop or a tablet especially if you take the bus or similar forms of commuting transportation going to school or to work. By doing so, you can get some work done even while you're still on the road. It need depends on the amount of personal space you can have while you're commuting. But by using technology to be more productive during your computing time, you can get the head start on many of your important tasks for the day while on your way to work or school. This would include catching up on your emails and other relatively simple tasks that don't require much thought. You can also use such gadgets for brainstorming.

Possibly the only disadvantage to switching from private transportation to public transportation is compromising travel time and reliability. For example, if driving normally takes in just 30 minutes to go to work or school, then riding the bus or the train we think you an extra 30 to 40 more minutes. But you can think of it in a more positive way. Instead of spending 30 minutes doing nothing but driving, you will be able to spend one hour to an hour and 10 minutes being productive while going to and from work or school. In which case, you will actually experience and net gain in terms of personal productivity.

Plan Ahead

You can always use our daily commuting time to plan out your day, regardless if you're using public or private transportation. Before leaving home you can already check your emails so you have more or less a good idea of the tasks that you need to plan out for the day. For this purpose, voice memos are very ideal. If you want to have an outline of your day in advance, you can use a voice memo to record your plan activities directly and without having to use your hands for listening to later as you officially start your work or school day. At the end of your day, you can also use this particular method to reevaluate and wind your productive day down and think about what you have done well for the day as well as those that you haven't. You can address any issues that may have gotten in the way with your being productive and plan on how to address the remaining challenges tomorrow.

Bike To Work

While it may seem like biking yourself to work maybe a big mistake, it may actually be a more productive alternative. Although it's a much slower way to get to work or school than, say, driving or taking the bus, it does have its advantages. For one, rush hours in most cities can be very, very bad - carmaggedon! As such, riding a bike can actually be a faster way of getting to work or school, if either isn't that far away from where you're living. It is also a more cost efficient way of going to and from school or work because you don't need to gas it up. And for those who are very particular about getting in the regular weekly exercises, biking to work is a very productive and efficient way of cutting down on commuting costs, getting to work on time and exercising regularly.

Word Of Caution

Just a word of caution, not all of these techniques or methods may work for you. It'll all depend on your personality, your situations, and the nature of your work as well as your own personal circumstances.

Carefully experiment with these to find out which will work out best for you to optimize your personal productivity while on the road.

Chapter 9: Multi-Tasking

Multi-tasking is the ability to think about and perform multiple tasks, duties, or actions at the same time. You may be familiar with the concept of walking and chewing gum at the same time – that is a basic form of multi-tasking.

The issue with multi-tasking is that the conscious brain is unable to focus on one particular task or action at a time. If, while the conscious brain is focused on this one task or action, and the subconscious brain is not able to effectively perform the second task or action effectively (sometimes called, 'muscle memory'), then it could essentially take more time to complete both tasks together than it would to complete them one at a time.

Multi-tasking can also increase the likelihood of errors or mistakes if not done properly. When your attention is split into two or more directions at a time, there is an increased probability that steps or details will be overlooked – sometimes, without any awareness.

And, multi-tasking has been shown to use up brain energy more quickly than focusing on one task or action at a time. Therefore, fatigue can come into play, slowing down your ability to function efficiently and effectively until you get the proper rest.

But, the good news is that you can train yourself to effectively multi-task, especially through planning and preparation.

As your learn skills, your mind expands through more connections between your brain's neurons. And, as those connections get stronger, the less you'll have to think about what you're doing.

The less you have to think about what you're doing, the easier it is to multi-task.

One key element to practicing and training to multi-task effectively is to take notes, or keep a log / journal. Take notes of ideas that come into your head, but that will distract you from your current focus. And, keep a log / journal of what you've completed versus what you still need to complete.

These two activities alone will help you maintain organization without taking away brain energy during the time of performance and action. They will also help you ensure that you're not overlooking or missing any steps or details.

In addition, when attempting to multi-task, do your best to group similar and related tasks (or, at least, non-conflicting tasks) together. This will keep your brain from spending too much energy switching between thought processes.

Another tactic to multi-tasking is to combine tasks that don't use much brain power. The tasks that do not require your full focus, aren't prone to vital errors, and / or that are relatively simple allow you to multi-task with minimal risk of mistakes or failure.

You can also time your tasks so that you're filling in pre-planned breaks of one task within another task.

But, remember that the brain and your active concentration can really only focus on one thing at a time.

Therefore, it's best to focus on one task completely then switch to the next one and focus on it completely – even if you're working on both of them within the same time period.

If you switch back and forth two quickly, you risk mistakes AND you can drain quite a bit of brain energy. So, give yourself enough time to adjust your mindset to the alternating tasks, and don't put too much pressure on yourself to achieve too much, too quickly.

It's all about balance.

Chapter 10: Dealing With Time Wasters

When you are working on your important tasks, you should not allow other people or events to divert your attention from what you need to do. If you give attention to time wasters, you will not get anything done. Here are some strategies on how you should deal with time wasters:

List your time wasters

To avoid giving attention to time wasters, you need to be aware of the unproductive activities that you do often. Most of the devices that distract us have notification sounds or visual signals that attract attention. These signals serve as triggers for our bad habits. When we hear them, our reaction is to automatically react to them. For most people, the reaction is to give attention to the source of the distraction and to spend time with it.

This is what happens when the phone rings or when it notifies us that we received an email. We habitually give attention to the source of the signal. The first step to stop these things from affecting your productivity is to be aware of them. You should go back to your time log and check when these habits happen. When you have identified the culprits, you should make a list of the habits that cause you to waste time.

Resist the urge to respond to distracting stimuli

As mentioned above, we have developed the habit of reacting automatically to notification stimuli. You can undo this habit by resisting the urge to divert your attention to the source of the notification signals. A ringing telephone, for instance, is impossible to ignore. If you plan to work continuously, you should tell all the people who may call you that you are will be temporarily unavailable to accommodate them. You can also let them go straight to voicemail.

You should do the same with other sources of distraction that have the tendency to take your attention away from your work. Some of the common sources of distraction are the television, smartphone apps, and unproductive tabs in the computer. You should remove them from your work area if you want to focus on your task. If this is not possible, you should learn to resist reacting to their notification signals.

E-mails should be checked only a few times per day. Learn to prioritize them in order of importance and respond accordingly. Keep your e-mail account organized and be sure to flag any junk e-mails so that you will not have to spend time going through and deleting them in the future.

Remove social media apps

Among the most common sources of distraction today are social media apps. They are in our phones and other mobile devices so we can carry them pretty much everywhere. If you notice that checking your social media accounts is taking too much of your time, you should remove these apps from your phone. These apps are designed to get your attention and to keep you hooked on them for long periods of time. You should remove them from any devices that you use for work.

Make your breaks boring

When mental and physical fatigue sets in because of work, most people feel that they need a reward. They seek activities that provide them with a mental or physical reward. The problem is that most of the rewards that we give ourselves are addictive. Over time, we develop a craving for the reward. There comes a point when we unknowingly overdo the rewarding part of the process.

The best way to prevent this is by identifying addictive rewards and replacing them with less exciting activities. For example, instead of logging on to your social media accounts during your breaks, you should just sit back and rest for a while. You could listen to music or meditate in silence.

When we take visually stimulating rewards, we often strain our senses with more information. Mental fatigue comes from the activity of taking in information, analyzing it, and creating an output. This is what we do when we work. However, we follow the same process when we are logged on to our social media accounts. As a result, the brain is still tired even after you are done with your break time.

For your breaks, you should pick activities that do not lead to mental fatigue. Meditation is one of the best activities that you can engage in to preserve your mental strength throughout the workday. It is relaxing and it improves your ability to focus.

Keep your environment tidy

A messy environment can also be a reason for wasting time. It is difficult to find things that we need if the surroundings are messy. You will also have some difficulty in moving around because of the mess. When put together, these small factors can cause you to waste a lot of time.

When tidying up, you need to create a space where you can move freely. You should practice the same principle at work and at home. If there are too many things lying around, you should consider reorganizing your space or giving some things away.

Prepare activities for waiting and commuting

Most people also consider traveling as a waste of time. Traveling is a time waster only if you do not do anything while you wait. For example, if you drive to work, you can listen to an audiobook while driving. This will allow you to catch up on your readings while on the road. If you love reading, you could also put digital books in your phone for those times when you are made to wait, like at the bus stop or train station.

If your job requires you to travel by air regularly, you should take advantage of the waiting time prior to boarding the airplane. Also, instead of just sleeping through your flights, you can do some productive activity that you can fit in the time.

Chapter 11: Stress-Free Productivity

Preparing your schedule while having optimal productivity in mind all the time can be a difficult task. Worrying about increasing efficiency and how to get everything done in time can work on the short term; however, there is a possibility that you will not stay committed to the method. And it is normal; people sometimes need a break from all this order.

But then after a while you start thinking: why did I put so much time and effort in this? There must have been a reason. And you decide to continue with it. You prepare a plan from which you expect the maximum results: increased productivity and an additional hour a day, just for yourself.

After the first day everything seems fine. The second day, your boss announces that you will have to work overtime this week, the same week that your daughter has a piano recital, which you will have to miss. All that effort disappears in a split second.

Not reaching the goals can bring additional stress in your life. In addition, all time management tricks were useless because of the unpredictable change in your schedule. Setting priorities for example don't do the trick anymore when you are physically unable to perform the task.

Few things can help you to overcome this. The methods for personal productivity enhancement and reduction of the stress caused by information overload will help you to stay prepared.

Collect Information

Your first step will have to include gathering information from the environment. Collecting every piece of information that catches your attention is crucial in this step.

Note down everything that is potentially relevant to your activities, whatever its subjects, degree or urgency, and importance might be. This will most likely include phone calls, emails, newspaper articles, suggestions from your coworkers, memories, and personal ideas.

Use one of the tools of extended cognition to collect all of this information. Notebook or electronic organizer will do the trick here. We will call this your In-basket.

However, collecting is just the first part of this phase. You will have to select what is of value for you by emptying the In-basket regularly. Deciding what to do with the gathered information will give you control over the collected materials. To be really efficien,t you will have to process and organize the items one by one.

Process and Organize

Being organized makes things easier in general. Imagine if you have to search for your socks at random places in your house every morning. Keeping them in a designated drawer makes it easier to find them and saves you a lot of time and frustration.

The same goes with your tasks, plans, goals, and to-dos. After emptying your In-basket, you will need to process the remaining information and decide what to do with it. The simplest and still efficient way is to combine them into categories. They should be based on the lowest common denominator; either time, location, or the priority level.

These categories will represent all of your Applicative files that will enable you to increase your efficiency and productivity. Not only that, they are designed for you to plan your future actions in the least stressful way.

They could look something like this:

Review

As in most of the projects, the reviewing phase is crucial. It will help you to stay in touch and improve in your daily routine, and better manage your weekly tasks.

The daily review must include your Calendar, with emphasis on the most important things you have to do on a particular day. The second part of it is reviewing the Action list, what you should do as soon as possible.

The weekly review should be an in-depth analysis of your Applicative files: In-basket, Calendar, Action list, Projects, Project plan, Waiting for, and Maybe. It is especially important to get an overview of what you need to do in the coming time period. Again, this will give you the feeling of control. This control, in addition, result in keeping all of your files up-to-date. This will include even the most tedious and seemingly unimportant work, such as cleaning out your email or your desk.

This kind of review is also important in order to develop and maintain trust in your new system. Feelings of clarity and purpose will accompany this action. Regular attempts to organize your files will also help you in unpredicted events. Changing circumstances can quickly ruin your long-term plan if you don't adjust your daily and weekly schedule.

Perform

At some point your will find all your lists up-to-date. What about now? How should you decide what to do first? There are four criteria that you should take in consideration.

Context

You probably can't do the same things when you are sitting at your desk as when you are walking in the park. The environmental context limits your choices and most probably defines your behavior. In the case that your Action list is long, it is advised to organize it by the context (home, office, outside). This will enable you to cluster the actions that can be performed in the same context.

Time availability

Time is always an issue. However don't push yourself. This won't help anybody. Fit the duration of your actions to the amount you actually have available.

Energy availability

The same thing goes for your energy levels. Sometimes you have to accept that you are tired and in need of a nap. Doing things by force could result in a low quality performance. Chances are that you will have to repeat the task which can set you back in your time and energy.

Priority

Regarding the context, as well as your time and energy, you will have to decide which things should be done first. The "Threefold model" for evaluating daily work can help you decide:

Your plan is set, your Applicative files are organized, even prioritizing doesn't seem a mystery anymore. The best thing now should be to start using these skills. However, your friend has a party tonight, and making this plan really precise would take a lot of energy and focus. Maybe it is better to do it tomorrow, when you actually have the will power to do it. Doing it today just wouldn't make sense.

This is where most of our time-management efforts start to collapse. Why are we so inclined to postpone our duties? Are we all just lazy or is there something more to it?

Chapter 12: Creating An Environment Where You Can Manage Your Time Wisely

Plain and simple, it will be impossible for you to manage your time wisely or focus on what you need to get done if you're in an environment that is not suitable for you in regards to getting work done. You'll notice that this statement is very broad and generic, but it only is because not all people will be able to manage their time the best in the same kind of environment. Just because one certain type of environment allows you to focus more on your work for you doesn't mean that it will for someone else, example.

So this step is all about how you can create an environment that will enable you to manage your time in the wisest manner. Again, we can't tell you exactly what kind of an environment you need for you, but we can suggest certain factors that you should take into consideration.

These factors are:

THE TIME OF THE DAY

It's not just the location of your environment that matters. It's the time of the day that you're in that environment. Do you work better in the morning and then like to rest during the afternoon, or do you find your mind to be more creative in the evenings? Only you know for yourself.

Granted, the time of day that you're in the environment may be dictated by your actual work hours, assume that you actually work in an office. But if you are self-employed or work from home, you'll have much more flexible in what time of day you focus most of your work on.

PRIVATE VS. PUBLIC

Are you more efficient in a room by yourself, or in an office or study area with multiple other people around you? Or do you like to work together in small groups? If you work better in groups, then you should ask any of your friends or colleagues if they would like to work alongside you, but if you work better by yourself and alone in a room then having your own office space would be better.

Remember that if you prefer to work alone but in a public setting, if you are self-employed or work from home, you have the opportunity to work in public locations such as libraries and coffee shops.

NOISE

While there's no denying that a lot of people prefer to work in an environment that is quiet with minimal distractions, not all people are this way. A library is a great example of a public location where you can work that's quiet; a coffee shop is also an excellent example of a public location that's noisier. At your office, do you like to work with the windows open and hearing the city life outside, or do you prefer to work with the outside world shut off? Again, whatever works for you is what you should go with.

Noise also doesn't just deal with the number of people conversing around you. It also deals with music. Some people are able to work much more efficiently if they are listening to relaxing music that they enjoy on their electronic devices. But again, other people need to have complete and utter silence in order to get things done.

POSTURING

Posturing refers to how you are physically when working. The overwhelming majority of people like to sit down at a desk or a table, with their back upright against the seat, in order to get work done. However, others like to lay down on a couch or exercise on a treadmill while tending to tasks.

You also need to ask yourself how long you are able to sit before you need to get up and move around. This will largely determine the number of breaks that you take in any given day.

Chapter 13: Set Your Goals

The first thing that you have to do in order to manage your time is to set your goals. Goals allow you to prioritize things that matter to you. Goals give you a strong sense of purpose and also allow you to focus your energy on things that matter. They enable you to separate the important tasks from those that aren't so important.

But, before you set your goals, you must determine the things that are important to you. You need to look inside yourself and determine your values and your desires. Take time to think what it is that you really want in this life. Do you want to be a successful businessman? Do you want to provide a good life for your family? Do you want to travel around the world? Do you want to raise good kids? Do you want to write a best-selling book? Do you want to earn at least one million dollars a year? Do you want to have exceptional academic achievement?

Then, after you determined your life's purpose, you need to set goals. Here are some tips that you can use in setting your goals:

1. You have to set goals that are aligned with your desire and purpose.

2. Make sure that you set goals for various parts of your life including finances, career, education, personal development, and relationships.

3. Set goals that are specific, measurable, attainable, relevant, and time-bound. It is great to set ambitious goals, but it is also important to make sure that these goals are achievable.

4. Set goals that motivate and inspire you to take action.

5. Write your goals. Unwritten goals have no power. Writing your goals on a piece of paper will compel you to take action to manifest your dreams into a reality.

6. Focus on activities that help you achieve your goals. This is how goal setting can help you manage your time. For example, if your goal is to travel around Europe and you need about $11,000 to do

that, you need to focus on activities that will allow you to raise that amount. So, instead of partying with your friends, you have to fill your schedule with money-making opportunities that will allow you to afford that trip.

Here's a table that can help you do this:

Goal: To raise $10,000 extra money to travel to Europe

Activities   Course of Action

Go to your regular 9-5 work and accomplish all your work-related task. You should keep this task or activity because this will help you raise money for your trip.

Meet with a potential business partner. You should keep this activity as a new business opportunity may also help you earn more money for the trip.

Go clubbing with your friends. You should discard this activity as this would not help you achieve your goal. Plus, it's an additional expense.

Of course, the table is just an example. But, this table can guide you in choosing the activities to keep and the activities to discard. Remember that you only have 24 hours every day. Your time is limited, so it is important to spend it on activities that really matter.

7.   Track your goals.

With all the distractions, it is easy to get sidetracked and lose sight of your goals. So, in order to achieve your goals and manage your time effectively, it is important to track your goals. You can use this by using goal management apps such as Goalsontrack, Nozbe, LifeTick, and Strides.

Steven Covey, the author of 7 Habits of Highly Effective People, said that you have to"begin with the end in mind". Remember that time is a limited resource so you have to spend it on things that matters to you. So, take time to set your life goals and then fill your days with activities and tasks that will help you achieve these goals.

Chapter 14: Time Management And Motivation

Lack of motivation is the cause of bad time management. If you keep putting things off because you don't feel like doing them, things just won't get done. But what if it would be possible to inject fun into the things you desire to do anyway? It is what time management motivation is all about.

To turn some difficult chore around, as it were, you need to take another look at it to see if there isn't something in it that you could enjoy doing. Let's say that you dislike housework. Okay, think of how good you will feel once it's done. Let's say you detest homework. Okay, think of how proud you will feel once it's all behind you.

Get friends involved in some of your tasks. You can't have them come over and clean house with you, but there are things that you could ask them to help you with. Being lighthearted about some things can make them less of a chore and more of a pleasing diversion. And your friends can help you achieve this.

Sometimes friends can be of assistance, but then so can some positive aspect added to a task. If doing homework is tiresome, try to turn on the radio to the classical music station and permit the sounds of music to help you through your reading or writing. This sort of background diversion is okay if it doesn't distract you from what you are trying to accomplish.

Another good way to think about time management motivation is to stop and reflect on the fact that doing a certain task is not the end of the world. It may not seem likely that comparing vacuuming with going to war is a good idea, but when you do this kind of comparison, the task at hand is not longer so terrifying. So do this kind of outrageous comparison whenever what you need to do needs to get done anyway.

In the end, it is important to reward yourself upon the completion of a job successfully. If you know that after vacuuming, for example, you can have a dish of ice cream, you are less likely to be grumpy. When you have some reward awaiting you after a chore, the chore becomes less of a burden.

It seems, therefore, that time management is not such a big affair after all. If you can keep things on the light side, you are going to get the best of time management motivation under your belt.

Chapter 15: Explore Ways To Work From Home

Make the most of your time working by reducing the activities that eat up the hours that you can spend doing more productive things. Depending on the type of work that you do, the industry you belong in, and the daily form of commuting that you undergo, you might want to explore different ways to work from the comforts of your own home.

If you have your own business, then deciding to work remotely is something you can choose to do instantaneously but the same cannot be said if you are part of a company. The thing about working from home is that it is not meant for everyone. It has its fair share of pros and cons that you have to acquaint yourself with to see if it really is the kind of professional arrangement that you can handle.

Here are some of the things that you can take advantage of if you do decide to work from home.

• Virtually zero commute. With your office being in your home, there is no need for you to spend valuable time waiting in line. Not only that, you save money as well and reduce part of your daily stressors which is another plus.

• You get to be more flexible as you are able to work when you are most productive - when you are in the zone. Being in clothes that are comfortable also helps boost your productivity as you won't be fidgeting every now and then in your corporate attire.

• Distractions can be reduced much easier. Not to say that there are no distractions at home but you have the ability to block these as you wish. You can set up an office in a quiet space far from where your kitchen, pets, or television set is.

• The balance between working and living can be achieved by working from home as well since your stressors are reduced and you gain more time to spend on more important things like family.

Working from home does have its fair share of cons though. This is why you should be mindful of what they are before you take that leap of faith.

• You must have a strong sense of self-discipline if you wish to work from home. This is easier said than done because without someone looking over your shoulder, you have a higher tendency to slack off. If you are not someone who can commit to working when necessary, then remote work may not be for you.

• Since you are working at home, there are no colleagues beside you to chat or collaborate with. Depending on your personality, this can get pretty boring at times and when we are bored we tend to procrastinate. The sense of isolation is something you have to work around if you wish to work from home. Another downside to working in isolation is the lack of exposure to collaboration and new professional connections.

• A benefit for your employer but not for yourself is the difficulty in shutting down after a day's work. When you work from home, there is the tendency to lose track of time so, in essence, you work longer hours. It is important that you learn to set a fixed schedule for your work. Start when you have to, take the allowable breaks in between, and then end the day as you would do in any other physical office.

• Ad hoc learning is limited when you work remotely because you are not constantly in face-to-face interaction with your peers. You may be communicating with them online but this is not enough for you to learn from your peers. If you decide to work from home, you should make an effort to seek additional learning opportunities.

Before you decide to work from home, there are certain questions that you have to ask yourself first. This kind of working arrangement comes with trade-offs and you should be amenable to them. You will indeed experience a higher level of comfort while working but it will require a stronger sense of responsibility and discipline in return. Here are some of the questions that you have to ask yourself to determine if you are remote work material.

1.   Are you someone who is organized?

For a remote working arrangement to work, you need to be as organized as possible. You have to have a place solely for work with only the materials that you need to do your job. This means that you should not work in the kitchen or in the entertainment area. You need to have a dedicated home office even if it is just a small one.

If you are handling multiple projects, you should have notes on each one. You need lists of tasks per project, contact personnel, reporting personnel, and so on and so forth. Failing to document your requirements per project is something you cannot afford to do.

You also have to know how to keep track of your responsibilities and their corresponding deadlines. It would be best if you kept a chart of things to do and a calendar for updates and progress evaluations. Maintaining communication with your colleagues is also important so you must have the tools to do so. Aside from a working phone, you should make use of online communication tools that allow for video conferencing, chat, and file sharing.

2. What kind of working environment best suits you?

If you are intent on not working inside an office, you can work remotely. Working remotely is not limited to working from home. You can actually work elsewhere - in a park, a coffee shop, the beach, anything that suits your fancy really.

It is best to ask yourself what kind of work environment suits your abilities. This means that you have to identify which setup works best in boosting your productivity. Other people cannot work at home because it distracts them from the things they need to do. There are others who work well inside libraries while their counterparts prefer coffee shops. Identify which environment fosters your creative mind and go with that.

3.   What kind of work process will you establish and apply?

If you will be working remotely, how will you ensure that you get the job done each and every time? You need to have a working process in play. This means that you need to think about a schedule for work including fixed hours in which your services will be rendered. You also have to figure out how to include your boss' and colleagues' needs into this process if you will be working collaboratively.

Part of your process should include deadline monitoring, deliverable submissions, and feedback or conference sessions. Just like the things that you need to involve yourself in when you work in an office setting, these should also be present in your work process if you decide to work from a different location.

There are plenty of opportunities that you can take advantage of if you wish to work remotely but keep in mind that this is not the kind of setup that works with everyone. Before you decide to try it out for yourself, see to it that you have what it takes to perform at your best and manage your time without the limitations and boundaries set by in-office working conditions.

Chapter 16: You Might Be Scheduling Your Time In The Wrong Ways

There are certain days when you feel like you have not achieved anything significant, even though you are tired from a busy working day in the office. With frequent interruptions, endless meetings, and urgent tasks, it is all too easy for this to happen. You can be busy the whole day without progressing on your high priority goals and projects. This is why you need to know how to properly schedule your time. There are several tools you can use to schedule your time. The easiest method is a pen and paper. Others include but are not limited to apps and software like MS Outlook, Google Calendar and Business Calendar. Find the right tool that suits your budget, personal taste, current job structure and your personal situation. Once you have decided on a scheduling tool, schedule your time like this:

*Identify the available time: The best approach is to start by designating work time i.e. the time you want to avail for your work. However, this will also depend on your personal goals and the design of your job. If you are pushing for a promotion for instance, you may want to put more hours in your work to show your dedication. On the other hand, if you are looking to spare some time for out of work activities, you will want to stick to your allocated hours, with no extension.

*Schedule important actions: Incorporate the actions you definitely have to undertake for you to do a good job. For example, if you are a manager, make sure you set enough time to deal with your team members' personal issues, supervision and coaching needs.

*Schedule top priority tasks: Go through your to-do-list and reschedule the urgent and high priority activities, including the essential maintenance errands that cannot be avoided or delegated. Let these appear at the time you are most productive during the day.

*Schedule contingency time: Incorporate some extra time in your schedule to deal with the emergencies and contingencies.

You can judge from your past experience how much time to allow.

*Schedule your discretionary time: The extra space left in your planner is the available time to achieve your goals and deliver your priorities. Go through your personal goals and prioritized to do list, analyze the time needed to achieve them and then schedule them in.

*Analyze your tasks: If you find that there is little or no time left for discretionary activities after scheduling your planner, go back through the previous steps and determine whether all the tasks outlined are absolutely necessary. You may find some tasks that can be handled in a more time efficient way, or even delegated.

Chapter 17: 5 Time Management Techniques

"Remember that time is money." – Benjamin Franklin

No matter how much time you cut down from different activities, you still find yourself wasting time in some way or the other. If that's the case, then you should get yourself back on track before you completely derail yourself, that is before you make a habit of these unnecessary time wasting.

It is important to learn proper time management techniques since early childhood; because by the time you grow up, you already have a good control over the clock. However, that's not the case with everyone; there are still many working professionals who see the clock only to be terrified that they have crossed their deadlines.

Learning proper time management will help you stay always ahead of the time and increase your productivity efficiently. Fortunately, for those who still wander in the darkness, not knowing anything about time management, a few simple time management techniques will help them find the light.

With these five simple time management techniques, you will be able to come out of the darkness and begin to do things efficiently. The only thing you need to do is follow them as much as possible.

Manage the work you have

As a working professional, there will be many projects that will be coming in, while you are working on one already. So, you keep them on your work desk, where it will eventually become dusty and forgotten.

Instead of simply putting it in your "to-do" list, go through the given work quickly; determine how much time and effort will be needed to complete that assignment. It will be much better if you use the Action Plan Matrix to prioritize it into its suitable category and then allot time for it or delegate it, if it can be delegated. Just decide the fate of that assignment instantly without putting it on a hold.

Organize them effectively

The curry you have prepared out of all the documents on your desk is the major problem. With so many documents here and there, it will take ages to find what you are looking for. Moreover, it is scientifically proven that having a clean working desk helps reducing stress and anxiety and gives you a clear mind to think about what to do next.

So, take some time off from your schedule and organize your documents into proper file categories. Separate them according to your work, personal reasons, bills to pay, or any other category you can think of. For example, if an important task which needs to be completed quickly, you can put it into "Urgent" file category. So the next time you choose which assignment you will complete next, take a look into your "Urgent" file. Your categories can be in this manner

- "urgent projects"
- "big projects"
- "small projects"
- "delegated projects"
- "bills to pay"
- "clients to contact"
- "completed projects"
- "pending payments"

Complete everything

So now you have an organized desk, where you can find everything you want easily. All you have to do now is to make time to complete them. If you wait until you have time then there is no way on earth that those projects will be completed, you must make time.

Check your schedule, prioritize your work, use time blocking and action plan matrix to divide the time you have in order to give time to every project. With correct planning, you can finish all the projects within the deadline. For those you cannot complete, delegate them if possible and the ones which require lot of time to complete, but gives low profit, simply eliminate them and use that time to do something productive.

Finish the ones with strict deadline

You will encounter many such tasks which have a very strict deadline. For example, you may have to register for a workshop, some bills to pay, renewing your driving license, drafting a check, etc. Mark these tasks with a not. Include these projects in your daily routine as you have to complete them that particular day if possible. Always treat the tasks with strict deadlines as priority and try finishing them before you are busy or distracted.

Remain calm and relax

If you follow these simple steps, there is no risk of missing a deadline. You don't have to continuously worry about the priority tasks or bills that have to be paid because you know that if they are urgent, you will be doing them first. When you know everything is going to be alright, there is no place for stress and frustration. Just be calm and relax.

With these simple time management techniques, you will be able to save a lot of time, which you can use to do something from your wish list, like learning a new instrument or watching your favorite TV shows or maybe visiting some hotel or cafeteria nearby.

Chapter 18: Techniques On How To Master Your Own Time

1.   Carry a schedule and record all your thoughts, conversations and activities for a week. This will help you understand how much you can get done during the course of a day and where your precious moments are going. You'll see how much time is actually spent producing results and how much time is wasted on unproductive thoughts, conversations and actions.

2.   Any activity or conversation that's important to your success should have a time assigned to it. To-do lists get longer and longer to the point where they're unworkable. Appointment books work. Schedule appointments with yourself and create time blocks for high-priority thoughts, conversations, and actions. Schedule when they will begin and end. Have the discipline to keep these appointments.

3.   Plan to spend at least 50 percent of your time engaged in the thoughts, activities and conversations that produce most of your results.

4.   Schedule time for interruptions. Plan time to be pulled away from what you're doing. Take, for instance, the concept of having "office hours." Isn't "office hours" another way of saying "planned interruptions?"

5.   Take the first 30 minutes of every day to plan your day. Don't start your day until you complete your time plan. The most important time of your day is the time you schedule to schedule time.

6.   Take five minutes before every call and task to decide what result you want to attain. This will help you know what success looks like before you start. And it will also slow time down. Take five

minutes after each call and activity to determine whether your desired result was achieved. If not, what was missing? How do you put what's missing in your next call or activity?

7.   Put up a "Do not disturb" sign when you absolutely have to get work done.

8.   Practice not answering the phone just because it's ringing and e-mails just because they show up. Disconnect instant messaging. Don't instantly give people your attention unless it's absolutely crucial in your business to offer an immediate human response. Instead, schedule a time to answer email and return phone calls.

9.   Block out other distractions like Facebook and other forms of social media unless you use these tools to generate business.

10. Remember that it's impossible to get everything done. Also remember that odds are good that 20 percent of your thoughts, conversations and activities produce 80 percent of your results.

Chapter 19: Get Organized

Do you know that an average American will spend a year of their life just looking for misplaced or lost items? In addition, on average we spend around 6 minutes in the morning looking for our keys.

Furthermore, are you aware that when you work on a messy desk, you spend on average 1 ½ hours every day being distracted by things; thus, out of sight out of mind and vice versa.

This goes to show that being organized is very important if you want to manage your time well. Therefore, no matter how good a time manager you are, if your organizational skills are lacking, you will never have enough time to complete tasks and achieve your goals.

Those 30 minutes you spend searching for a document counts. Apart from stealing your time away, disorganization is also very costly. It could drastically affect your productivity and negatively influence your physical and mental health. For instance, most people simply have a hard time concentrating on something if they are unable to find something they really wanted. Therefore, organization is especially important at helping you remain in control of your time all through the day. Here are a few tips that will help you with organization:

Use a Pocket Notebook to Capture Thoughts: Get a portable notebook where you can write down your thoughts throughout the day as you work. Disorganization of the mind is a very serious thing that most people ignore. It wastes your mental energy! If your thoughts are here and there, your actions will be disorganized as well. Get a notebook and use it to organize your thoughts daily.

Spend Brief Time Every Day Organizing: 15 minutes is a reasonable time you should dedicate to preparing your To-do list and getting a solid grasp of what your day is going to look like. Doing this everyday will save you time, the in-between tasks time you spend trying to figure things out.

Clear Your Table: It is common for your desktop/work station to clutter as you work during the day; while this may be, clutter is very distracting. Sometimes, you cannot see the effect it has on you because often, the effects of clutter are mental.

Always keep your desktop/work station clean, clear, and free. Do not use it as a storage space; instead, use the drawers or get a box or other storage solutions for your files and other important work materials. Every morning before you start working for the day, clear out your desk.

Create an Action Area on Your Desk: Before you start any task, whip out everything you need to complete the task and place them on a designated area of your desk. After completing each task, get rid of the item related to it. This will make it easy to have access to all the resources you need to complete tasks without interruptions.

Create An Effective Filing System: If you do not already have a filling system, create one. Create files for all your documents and use storage boxes for all your tools. This makes it easy to access items you need. If you do not like having too much paper, you could digitalize your documents by scanning them and storing them on electronic devices.

Organization is very important; devote time to getting organized. Not doing so could cost you a lot of money, time, well-being, productivity and of course, career or personal advancement.

Chapter 20: How To Find More Time In Your Day Than You Think You Have And Accomplish Your Goals Faster

Time management is a huge hurdle to overcome at any point in one's life. There are a few main points essential to accomplishing this, and they will be discussed in this chapter.

1. Set realistic goals.

Controlling your goals increases the probability achieving them. For example, it might be easier for you to hone your skills at a certain task rather than becoming a company CEO. Also, if you cram too many activities within the day, you may get frustrated or feel too rushed. Be realistic about the number of tasks per day and the amount of time you allot per task. Challenge yourself, but know your limits. Success can be achieved by accomplishing one small goal at a time.

2. Prioritize.

You have to know what's important and finish these tasks first. It's better to focus on and accomplish key tasks early because this will give you enough time for less important tasks afterward.

3. Organize.

Organization plays a central role in time management because this helps you finish goals faster and more efficiently. You need to organize what needs to be done and when they need to be finished. You could set up daily or weekly calendars to achieve these, but be sure to stick to only one calendar to avoid wasting time remembering where you wrote a certain reminder. If not, you may opt to synchronize all of your calendars so you always have one list of activities wherever you look.

4. Know when you're most productive.

Try keeping a time log for a week or two and determine at which time period you have the greatest energy or could finish a greater amount of tasks. This period is the best time for you to accomplish demanding tasks, such as projects and papers. Other times, you may reserve for less challenging activities, like doing errands.

5. Use transition time wisely.

Time wasted on commuting or waiting in line can actually be a good resource. During these times, you could try doing something productive. You could learn a new language, or even read a book! Using this normally wasted time creates time for things you actually want to do.

6. Start working.

People oftentimes get spend too much time planning that they have no more time to actually work. Sometimes, the best course of action is to actually start already. While working, you'll figure out what needs to be done and how. Even if you have to repeat a few steps, you'll still have a head start because you're working and not waiting.

Chapter 21: Myth

Say "Yes" To Every Opportunity

Please don't. Occasionally, work the muscles in your mouth, align them for a common purpose and give life to the word: No. I can tell you the pillars holding the world will not suddenly crumble if you do.

You want to be liked. You want people to love you and gush about what a great person you are. But ask yourself; what is so great about a person that lives all of their lives for others; their opinions, their wants, their whims and caprices, everything.

It is even sadder, because in trying to be amenable even when you know it is inconvenient for you, you will end up doing the very thing you tried so hard to safeguard against; hurt your growth and negatively impact on your relationships, personal and business.

Of course, you should try to help people, but never at the detriment of what you know to be your limits. If someone asks you to carry out a task for them and you know you simply do not have the extra time to, say no politely but firmly. They will understand, and even if they don't, you would have done the right thing for you and them. Saying maybe or a tentative yes would be raising their expectations even when you know there is every possibility you might be unable to fulfill it.

If that happens, they will be disappointed, and you will be miserable.

The human mind is an amazing entity. If you commit yourself to a task you know very well you do not have the luxury of time to carry out, you set yourself up for a fail from the onset. This is because it becomes a bone that is stuck half-way down your throat. You agonize over the things you need to adjust so you can create time for it, even though you very well know that time just isn't there. Or you try to device creative ways with which you can get out of the inconvenient commitment. This agonizing and rearranging takes time, time that could have been better channeled into actually being productive and getting things done.

Your brain burns energy and your brainpower is depleted. And all for what?

When you're an all the time yes person, slowly you begin to lose the essence of self and forget the things that are actually yours; your opinions, identity, and capacity.

Be polite about it, be humane, and give reasons if you can, about why it is a bad idea for you for you to take on additional responsibilities at that point in time.

"When I claim more than I can handle, I limit the opportunities for another person in my community." – Jeff Shinabarger.

It is much more profitable to under promise and then delivers above expectations. It would make another's life easier and make you feel good about yourself.

Most importantly, remember to live for you. The truth is people will always need something from you and another is that limited resource that you are, it will be impossible to meet those needs all the time. So do what you can, in a way that does not negatively impact on you.

Do it because it is what you want to do, and not because it is what you are expected to do. Maybe you will be disliked, judged or rejected, but in all of it, you will have the knowing that above all, you were true to yourself.

Myth: E-mail Is The Most Effective Way To Communicate

Over the years, the culture of sending and receiving email has become the number one form of communication at the workplace. No doubt, it is a great tool for keeping electronic records of incoming and outgoing messages.

But saying it is the most effective is to put it simply, stretching the truth. Emails have become time vampires, sucking away a huge portion of the work day.

Some people have cultivated the habit of replying to emails in real time. It doesn't matter whether they receive 20 emails in an hour; they are going to reply to all immediately as they come in. Pray tell, how much time is left to do the actual work of the day? Very little time, because fielding emails takes away from the mental energy that can be better channeled to other tasks leaving you tired even when you haven't gotten a lot done.

There are ways to manage emailing. Avoid the need to respond to emails as they come in. Instead, create blocks of time in your day dedicated to all things email. It could be twice in the day; in the mornings when you get to work and evenings just before you log out for the day. That way, you get to attend to your emails while ensuring the other aspects of your work do not suffer.

Available statistics show that over 2.6 billion people in the world used email in 2016, with an average of over 100 mails being sent at work alone. For every email sent, received and responded to, there is an equivalent time that could be channeled more productively being flushed down the drain, never to be gotten back and effectively killing productivity.

It is good; the desire to want your finger on the pulse of happenings, but it is also dangerous in that your inbox becomes a marketplace of different threads and notifications that require you to expend more time trudging through.

Sending an email with proper and acceptable grammar is as important as sending one that is concise and gets straight to the heart of the matter. Rambling while sending a mail wastes not only the recipient's time, but also yours, time that could have been better spent tackling high priority tasks.

Personally, I use Slack. I find it a very valuable tool in communicating with my team and members, and in enhancing quick communications and collaborations. In fact, it is sometimes described as an email killer. Slack claims its users report receiving 48.6% less internal email after they commenced use of the tool.

That is great, isn't it? The less time spent on sorting through and responding to email, the greater time that can be focused on productivity.

Chapter 22: Effective Technological Tools To Help You Manage Your Time

In the past, practically everything had to be done manually. Letters were handwritten, mail was sent through the post office and documents had to be edited and recopied manually. But at present, thanks to the recent advancements in technology, all these can be done easily and effortlessly. There is a vast selection of tools, both electronic and paper-based, that can improve productivity and help save precious time. Before you start investing on these tools, however, you have to consider the following questions:

1.   Do you need it?

This is the most essential and vital question that you need to answer when thinking about buying a time management tool. A lot of people spend money on items and gadgets that they do not actually need just so they could keep up with the latest trends. This is not only a waste of money but can also use up your time (e.g. excessive use of a smartphone for social media) instead of saving it. The best way to know whether you need a particular tool is by weighing its potential pros and cons.

2.   What features are necessary?

The main reason why gadgets sell is because of the features that they possess. Lots of gadgets can now perform a multitude of functions. However, not all of them are beneficial to the user. In truth, as suggested by the Pareto Principle, perhaps only 20% of these features account for 80% of your usage. Thus, when contemplating on buying a time management tool, you have to determine which model or make has all the key functions you are looking for but not too much that you do not need. You also have to know if any of those features would come in handy. Reading reviews and articles and getting the input of your colleagues might be helpful in the decision-making process of choosing a time management tool.

3.   Is it user-friendly?

With the incessant technological improvements of tools come several complications and advanced features. Typically, the more high-end a product is, the harder it is to work out. If you want to take on complex tools, you first have to learn how to utilize them appropriately. Since these tools are supposed to help you with time management, it is impractical to spend too much time and effort figuring out how to use it. Hence, it is imperative that you choose a tool that is user-friendly and in line with your skill level.

4.   How dependable is the tool?

Reliability is crucial when buying a time management tool. Breakdown and malfunctions not only consumes time but also causes a great deal of stress. Durability should be highly considered before investing on any tool. Also, opt for a maintenance contract when buying so that your unit will have a warranty in case it needs to be repaired. Also, keep a backup unit in place in the event of malfunction or breakdown.

5.   Will it be easily outdated?

Living in the age of technology, it is hard not to be frustrated with the unending upgrades and developments of certain devices. In a matter of months, companies can come up with better versions of any gadget that you currently have. Before you know it, your units would be outdated and obsolete. So, if you intend to buy a new tool, you need to make a thorough research about the different models and figure out whether that tool will still be functional in a few years.

By answering these questions, you can then gauge the worth of a device and how compatible it is to your time management techniques.

Effective Time Management Tools

Today's generation has been highly reliant on technology. In fact, most businesses cannot do without different technological devices in their offices. While there are several gadgets to choose from, there are two main technological devices that are highly time-saving – personal computers and the smartphones or personal digital assistants.

1.   Personal computers

Computers are vital to any business. At present, practically anything can be done digitally using a computer. Some of the important features of a personal computer are:

•   High-speed internet – save for a few pre-installed programs, a computer would virtually be useless without an internet connection. Through the internet, you can send e-mails, do research and perform several other functions.

- High memory and spacious hard drive – a computer operates faster when it has a lot of free memory and hard drive space.

- Data compression program – if your computer has a reasonable memory capacity and hard drive space, this program will be useful. It reduces the size of files, resulting to higher hard drive space.

- Up-to-date software – do this for software that you religiously use. Updates are often free of charge so take advantage of the improvements that come with the upgrade.

- Printer – if you are in the workforce, more often than not you will need to print documents on a regular basis. Having your own printer will give you the opportunity to work from your home and not having to rely on the office printer before you can work on your tasks.

The following are tips for using the personal computer in order to make it an effective time management tool:

- Erase unused folders and files.

Delete documents, programs and other files that you know you will not be using anytime soon. This not only frees up hard drive space but also helps you keep your important files and folders organized.

- Only install software and programs that you need.

Each program installed in your computer consumes memory and can ultimately affect the computer's speed and performance. Get rid of those that you do not need or will not use. If you do not know how to uninstall, ask help from someone who does. In the long run, this will save you a lot of time.

- Keep a back up of your data.

It is possible for you to lose all of your data in a flash. This could be due to malfunctioning or an unattended virus. Regardless, always make sure that you save all your files using backup systems such as external hard drives, USBs or CDs.

• Train yourself to use the basic functions of the programs you will use.

When using a program, make sure that you know all the basics. That way, you will not dissipate time trying to figure out how the software works. Also, try not to get too caught up on the other unnecessary features of your programs. There is a time for trying out new things but not when you are in the middle of performing a task. If you have free time, you may tinker with the different functions of a program.

Other variations of the personal computer are laptops and tablet PCs. The laptop is basically a smaller version of a computer with a relatively smaller hard drive space. That, however, will not be much of a problem if you only intend to write documents or surf the Internet. The laptop is compact and wireless; you can carry it around and bring it with you wherever you go. The tablet PC, on the other hand, is a portable type of computer that has a touchscreen and numerous applications. These are not ideal for saving large files because they do not have high memory space.

2.   Smartphones and personal digital assistants

Before the emergence of smartphones, the personal digital assistant, or simply PDA, was the most advance technological method of organizing and planning out tasks. From the name itself, it is a digital version of a secretary. It is also called a pocket PC because it is a small device that fits in your pocket but has nearly all the functions of a personal computer. Having a PDA meant that you have everything you need in one compact tool. But when the smartphone was introduced a few years ago, the PDA was pretty much rendered obsolete. To date, there are still a few manufacturers of PDAs but they are not as appealing as they once were.

Both devices have their respective pros and cons. On one hand, the PDA is cheaper and carrier independent. On the other hand, smartphones function both as a PDA and a mobile phone, can utilize both wi-fi and cellular data, a collection of applications and programs to choose from and faster operating systems. Despite the differences between the two gadgets, they also possess a number of similarities. These features are fundamental and are ones that you need to manage your time:

- Compact size

One of the desirable features of both the smartphone and PDA is their size. Having all the necessary things you need in one device is highly practical, allowing you to bring it with you anywhere without carrying too much items. Also, by having it with you at all times, you can constantly check for important things to do such as messages that you need to respond to.

- Scheduling feature

This is arguably the most important feature of the devices. This tool will allow you to record appointments, events and important reminders within the system, ensuring that you will not miss any important deadlines or meetings.

• Database and address book capacity

These gadgets' address books serve as your database. The address book features multiple fields where you can input information such as mobile number, e-mail address, office and home address, etc.

• Search feature

This feature is simple but useful. When you end up saving a memory in the device and somehow misplace it, you may easily locate it through search feature.

• Cut, copy and paste capability

These features save a lot of time and makes post-it notes seem archaic. Using these capabilities, you may transfer any information from one segment of your device to another with just a few clicks of the button.

- E-mail client

Electronic mail is perhaps the fastest and most convenient method of relaying messages and sending important files. Having an e-mail client on your device not only permits you to send messages from literally anywhere, it also enables you to receive mails that you normally would not get to read instantaneously unless you are in front of your computer. It is an efficient way to stay in the loop.

- Expense records

Using this section, you can construct a number of systems used to keep track of your personal and business expenditures.

There are still others who prefer paper-based tools such as planners, post-it notes, notebook organizers, actual calendars, index cards and to-do lists. This works particularly well for people who are not tech-savvy. You may choose to employ these methods provided that you can do it quickly and effectively. Otherwise, you may need to utilize more advanced technological tools instead.

Time management tools are just a small part of a bigger picture. On its own, these tools can do little to help you control your time. When used with other strategies, it could effectively improve your productivity and assist you in accomplishing your time management goals and objectives.

Chapter 23: Making Time For You

Efficient time management is a widely accepted key factor for institutions such as schools, companies and systems. It is incorporated to be more efficient for service delivery when referring to businesses as a whole, as well. Another common and accepted fact of time management, is that it is a limited resource. This is because if time is lost, it can never actually be replaced.

As a result, it is often the case that time is minimal or simply unavailable. Therefore, diminishing the ability to do everything that you'll need to do, in a given frame of time. This may lead to a build-up of pressure from unattended work, that may end up causing stress on the person. As an example, it may occur at the point when you are preparing for examinations, or amidst finalizing your calendar for the year; when you need to consolidate the pressure of serious study with discovering time to apply for jobs.

Excellent time management can be especially essential. When we have identified the means by which we can enhance our time management, we can start to alter our schedules and patterns of behavior, to diminish any time-related stressors within our lives. As a result, we will learn that time management skills are quite important in today's busy world.

There are different approaches towards achieving time management success in our lives. These different approaches all have concrete and sound arguments. We will outline these different approaches together with examples and tips, for achieving effective time management skills, exponentially.

The Clock Time Approach

The dictionary defines time as, "The indefinite proceeded advancement of presence and events before, present and future, viewed as a whole."

In general terms, there are 2 types of time: clock time and relative time. In clock time, there would be 60 seconds in a minute, the 60 minutes would aggregate into an hour, 24 hours would amount to a day and finally 365 of these days would sum up into a year. Unequalled passes similarly. When somebody turns 50, they are precisely 50 years of age, no more or no less.

The Real Time Approach

In real time, time is considered to be relative. Time drags or flies by, according to the activity that you are performing at the time. Two hours at a railway station waiting for a train, can feel like 10 years! Yet a 10-year-old child may play in a playground for the same amount of time, which seems like 20 minutes!

This approach argues the fact behind time management methods and practices; pertinent to clock time comparison. It argues that individuals do not live in clock time but they operate in a real time scenario, a place in which time usually passes by swiftly or slowly. So, either when you are you are really enjoying yourself, or finding that time drags to the point of unending slowness, for example, when you are sick or working in a job you don't enjoy.

Time management skills that rely on real time are quite easy to master as it is only a certain mentality that inhibits progress. It exists in both your conscious and subconscious mind. You are its creator, and as a result, it is actually fairly easy to manage it. It's an easy approach to master which really works, when executed correctly. The only recommendation for a person using this approach, is to remove any limitations that you may have placed on yourself. It is also necessary to remove any self-inflicting sabotaging behaviors that you may have around yourself. Including: people, places, habits or things.

In the real-time approach, there are three ways to spend time. These are thoughts, dialogues and your vivacity. Therefore, your time management system will be centered upon these three components:

1. Any action or discussion that is critical to your success ought to have a period designated to it. "To do" lists get longer and more to the point where they can

become truly workable. Plan appointments with yourself and make time abstracts for highly needed contemplations, discussions, and activities. Make arrangements for the time when they will commence and finish. Have the self-control to keep these arrangements, regardless of anything else, unless your health or wellbeing denotes changes.

2. Carry a diary schedule and record every one of your ideas, interactions, and activities for that week. This will help you see the amount of work or effort you can complete - over the span of a day. Then gauge or investigate where and how you are spending valuable minutes. You'll perceive the measure of the time period that is invested in achieving results, and the amount of time that is being squandered on inefficient contemplations, discussions and/or activities. This includes social media and texting too. Allocate a time for these, if you cannot live without them.

3. Plan to spend no less than half of your time occupied with contemplations,

exercises and discussions that produce the majority of your outcomes.

4. Do plan time for mishaps and interruptions. Arrange for time to be pulled away from what you're doing. For example, the idea of having "office hours." Office hours are just another way of saying, "arranged interferences."

5. Take the initial 30 minutes daily to arrange your day. Try not to commence your day until you are sure of what you have planned for your time during the day. The most critical time of your day is the time you plan... to plan your time! You can reread that because it will make sense, and it is super important to reinforce this.

6. Take five minutes before each planned task, and assign quick bullet points/thoughts to decide what result you need to accomplish, by the end of it. This will help you to recognize what your end goal achievement looks like before you even begin. What's more, it will keep you organized and feeling accomplished. Take five minutes after every task, and figure out if your planned result was

accomplished. If not, contemplate what you might have missed, and how you would rearrange that task better, next time.

7. Put up a "do not disturb" mark online, when you need to complete work in a given time frame. This will minimize any interruptions you might have during the allocated time.

8. Practice not looking at your phone when it's ringing or as messages come in. Remember, just because they appear, you can wait for the allocation time to arrive. Deactivate instant messaging. Don't instantly flash your attention to them, unless it's vitally significant to your business, to offer a prompt human response. Rather, plan a period to answer emails and return phone calls, daily as required.

9. Remember it is quite hard to execute all required tasks in full. Moreover, it is important to note that chances are that approximately 20 percent of your contemplations, interactions and activities

will yield only 80 percent of your expected outcomes.

Working Smarter Not Harder

This approach tries to negate the idea that, for an individual to use time wisely they need to be hyper-productive. It actually argues that hyper-productive people who switch from task to task, (always checking their emails, organizing events, or running activities), do not necessarily have successful lives, in terms of goal achievement and orientation.

This is mainly due to their poor time management tendencies because hyper-productivity can easily lead to unreal productivity noted as: a consistent need to do something and a likelihood to throw away precious time on trivial activities or tasks.

Instead of being hyper-productive, one should seek to work smarter, and not harder. An individual should always try to be contemplative in the thinking process and always ask how a task can be done more effectively, or even eliminated altogether.

Proper time management is achieved by simplifying how work is done, doing tasks faster and relieving work pressure. It's not just about squeezing as many tasks into your day as possible. I promise you — there really are enough hours in a day for everything you'd like to do, but it may take a bit of rearranging and re-imagining first of all.

1. Finish your most essential assignments first.

Every day, distinguish a few tasks that are the most vital to finish, and do them first. Always do the least enjoyable tasks after that. So, as the day progresses the tasks become more enjoyable, and less vitally important.

2. Figure out how to say, "no."

Making a ton of time for sentimental duties can result in you doing too much and eventually becoming overly stressed. To be clear, you have to figure out how to decline some opportunities. Your target ought to be: to go up against only those duties that you know you have time for, and that you genuinely think are vital to your cause.

3. Rest no less than 7 hours.

A normal human being needs 7 hours of rest for their body and brain to work ideally.

4. Dedicate your whole mind to the job that needs to be done.

Locate a tranquil work environment, or listen to some out music that inspires or relaxes you.

Lay off any distractions and focus on the job that needs to be done; that is allocated. Nothing else ought to exist. Inundate yourself in it.

5. Start doing tasks early.

It's so much more pleasant and less stressful to get an early start on something.

6. Try not to permit insignificant points of interest that drag you down.

Do not focus on past mistakes or what you've done in the past. One greatly improves him or herself from pressing forward, getting the tasks finished, and meditating on things a short time later. Allocated time for thought and contemplation is vitally important.

7. Transform key undertakings into propensities.

Whatever key tasks you are performing, are more manageable if you form them as a habit. This can only be done if you do it regularly, though. Moreover, with time it will develop into a normal and enjoyable undertaking.

8. Be conscious about the measure of TV/internet/gaming time.

Become more mindful about the amount of time you spend on these exercises. Essentially, you can do this by seeing how much time they're sucking up, and then you'll start to do them less.

9. Depict a period limit in which to finish an errand.

Rather than simply guessing the time it takes to complete a task and considering the unending statement, "I will be here until this is done!" Actually take a stab at the definitive number of hours it will take (in weeks, days, hours, and minutes).

Practice putting a time constraint on all tasks you are doing. This will push you to focus on being more productive, regardless of the fact that you may need to go back and include more time later on.

10. Leave a buffer time between assignments.

Permitting ourselves break-time between errands need to be done, can be a much-needed refresher for our brains. While taking a break, go for a short walk, ponder, or play out some other mind-clearing exercises, so that you use the time to relax and refresh your body and mind, as a necessity.

11. Try not to think about the totality of your schedule.

You need to understand that no measure of thought will make your schedule of tasks any shorter.

The only thing that can be done is to spotlight on the one undertaking that is before you.

12. Eat healthily and Exercise.

The above additions are linked well with working efficiently. They improve your energy, refresh your mind, and permit you to contemplate all the more effortlessly.

13. Do less.

This is a strategy suggested by one of my most loved bloggers, Leo Babauta. Fundamentally, do less is another method for saying, "Do the things that truly matter."

Calm down and identify tasks that should be done, and focus on those things. Do fewer things that make more esteemed outcomes, instead of more things that are generally trivial.

14. Use weekends, but only a bit.

Doing some tasks on weekends can truly diminish the workload during the week, while still availing yourself spare time for weekday activities.

15. Sort out organizing frameworks.

Being organized enables you to gain huge amounts of time. Make a filing framework for reports. Ensure all things have a spot to be stored safely.

16. Accomplish something during waiting times.

Discover constructive things to do during waiting time. Like when you get put on hold, or while your computer is starting up, for the day.

17. Lock yourself in.

This ensures no distractions. In some cases, the main way one can complete something is to stay focused on the task at hand. Do not allow people or things into your work space, if possible.

18. Bundle up related undertakings together.

Distinctive undertakings need diverse sorts of considering, so it bodes well to permit your brain to keep on flowing with its present zone of thought, as opposed to changing superfluously to something that is going to oblige you to re-arrange. Keep it simple, and focused.

19. Discover time for stillness.

Finding time in your life for quiet and the addition of non-movement actually decreases nervousness, and demonstrates to you that there is no compelling reason to always surge ahead relentlessly. It additionally helps to ease pressure from work and makes it more pleasurable, too.

Chapter 24: Creating A System

Eliminating procrastination is just one part of Time Management. The next step is to actually divide your time into sections and assign productive activities to each one that will contribute towards a common goal. The problem with most people is that they know what they're supposed to do BUT they don't know exactly where to place it in their day.

Should they wash the dishes first or do the laundry?

Should you write your Economics paper first or start with the Human Rights reaction paper?

Creating a system essentially lets you set up an order of priority so that you'll know exactly which ones can and must be done first. Here's a guide that should help you:

Routines and Not Routines

First things first, it's important to differentiate between the routines and the ones that aren't. Routines are those that you do on a daily basis, a weekly basis, monthly, or basically anything that's repeated over a certain course of time. Perfect examples are cleaning the house, finishing your paperwork, filing your taxes, or even exercising. It's important to note which ones are routine so that you can easily place it in your schedule and turn it into a rhythm or a series of chores rather than just one chore.

Creating Your Rhythm Routine

This essentially means a series of task that you permanently string together as part of your daily routine. Think of how notes are stringed together into a piece of music so that they sound incredibly good when played together. Your Rhythm Routine follows the same analogy is that form habits done at the same time each day at the same order.

Here's an example:

• You wake up in the morning, stretch your legs and open the curtains to let the light in.

• You fix the bed

- You make coffee and while it brews, you make breakfast
- You eat breakfast and immediately wash the sink
- While there, you wipe the table and the kitchen counters
- You brush your teeth
- You clean the house
- You take a bath and get ready for work

You're probably thinking: this is something I do every day! Well of course, and chances are you've perfected the pattern into an art form. The routine is so familiar to you that you probably don't make coffee until you've fixed the bed. Or perhaps you don't brush your teeth until you've cleared the skin, the counter, and the kitchen table.

These are all small habits that make up a pattern – and we tend to ignore it because it's so familiar to us. What you don't realize however is by taking these activities as part of a 'package' rather than individually, there's little chance that you'd skip one. If you're so used to cleaning the house before going to work — then you'll be sure to have it cleaned before walking out that door.

This is what we mean by "Rhythm". If you want to add a new habit or activity that you tend to delay or procrastinate on — there's a higher chance that you'd do it if you place it smack in the middle of a Rhythm. For example, you can exercise in between fixing the bed and making coffee. By adding this activity into your Rhythm, you'll be compelled to perform the task; otherwise you won't "advance" to the next part of the routine.

Obviously, there are some pitfalls to this approach starting with a blatant disregard to order. Even with a routine firmly in your mind, you can still talk yourself out of exercising and just go straight to what you're supposed to do next. This is why…

30 Day Challenge

You should challenge yourself into doing the hated activity for 30 days straight. If you skip one, you start the count all over again. Why 30 days? Studies show that if you manage to hold onto a habit for 30 straight days, there's a very good chance that the habit becomes a permanent one.

Logistics

The Rhythm Routine is much more effective if you apply logistics into the equation. Essentially, this means putting together a sequence of events in such a way that it becomes easier for you to do them. For example, your Rhythm Routine is to first arrange breakfast followed by fixing the bed and then drinking coffee before finally taking a bath for work.

The logic of the Rhythm is offbeat because you're making things harder for you. You're already in your room – why wouldn't you fix the bed first and THEN prepare breakfast? Simply put, there should be a natural progression in your Rhythm so that the first task and second task have the shortest distance against each other.

Do the X Technique

Use the calendar to make the 30 day challenge more compelling for you. Put an X mark on every day that you've managed to successfully complete your rhythm without skipping anything. Use a bright red marker and make that X really big so that it occupies the whole box. You might be surprised at how this little thing can make a change in your motivation. Many people stick to their ideal routine simply because they don't want to break the string of bright red X marks on their calendar. Somehow, it's a very visual reminder of a goal that can discourage you from mismanaging your time with procrastination.

What About Non Routine Stuff?

When it comes to the non-routine tasks, a different approach must be taken. These are essentially those things that you only have to do once or every now and then. They're important and sometimes urgent, but they're not part of your daily existence. A good example would be writing a report for school or finishing up some paperwork at the office.

Post and Pin

For non-routine stuff, the most basic technique is to "post and pin". All you need is a post it note and a corkboard or even just a blank wall that you look at often. A lot of people do this, but it's often ineffective because they don't use it right. For example, don't just write what you're supposed to do. Instead, also write WHEN you're supposed to do it and perhaps add a little smiley face on the bottom to give you that little bit of motivation. For example: pick up laundry, November 27, Sunday.

By having a date, the deadline becomes more real to you. You can now quantify it so that you can easily include it in your schedule for that particular day.

Arrange by Priorities

When it comes to non-routine stuff, it's a good idea to arrange them by priorities. Is it better to study for your exam first or should you finish that paper before studying? Should you clean the bathroom first or start with the bedroom?

Priority arrangement is strongly dependent on when you need to get the job and the repercussions if you don't get it done on that particular time. For example, you need to write a paper on Thursday but you also need to pay your utility bills on the same day. Failure to write your paper could mean failing the subject. However, if you don't pay your utility bills – you'll have to pay an additional amount for penalty.

It falls down to a cost-benefit analysis which allows you to decide which risks are worth taking and which aren't. There are techniques today that teach you how to approach tasks which will be discussed later.

Assign Deadlines

It's been said that a goal without a deadline is just a dream – and this can be applied to Time Management as well. You might tell yourself that you need to finish your paper on Economics but unless you place a deadline on that paper, you'll never going to start putting words to paper. This is why it's a good idea to quantify your goals. How many hours do you need to get something done? When should you start and when should you stop? When should the paper be ready?

Conclusion

I hope you like this book. If you liked the book; kindly review the book.

About The Author

David Tracy & Brian Allen are amazing friends born with the vision to promote the art of productivity among the masses. The authors have written several research papers on the topic. David has served as an instructor promoting various cultural arts in University of San Francisco. He is currently living with his spouse in Texas.

Brian is a consultant manager.

CPSIA information can be obtained
at www.ICGtesting.com
Printed in the USA
BVHW071301291121
622787BV00022BA/357